In Society

'IN SOCIETY'

The Brideshead Years

NICHOLAS COURTNEY

PAVILION
MICHAEL JOSEPH

First published in Great Britain 1986 by
Pavilion Books Limited
196 Shaftesbury Avenue, London WC2H 8JL
in association with Michael Joseph Limited
27 Wrights Lane, Kensington, London W8 5DZ

Designed by Lawrence Edwards

Typeset by The Word Factory, Rossendale, Lancashire

Printed and bound in Great Britain by
Butler & Tanner Ltd, Frome, Somerset

British Library Cataloguing in Publication Data
Courtney, Nicholas
In society : the Brideshead years.
1. Upper classes——Great Britain——History——
20th century   2. Great Britain——Social life
and customs——20th century
I. Title.
941.082′0880621   DA566.4
ISBN 0–907516–91–2

For Vanessa

Contents

Illustrations

INTRODUCTION

*A*GES OF GREAT CHANGE PRO-
duce either nostalgia or euphoria. The nostalgia can take a
gentle, golden-hued form that adheres to the memories of a past
age and hopes to preserve, at the very least, its style and manners
– 'The good old times – all times when old are good'.(1) It may
also come in the form of disapproval, an urge to stamp on the
rising tide, whatever the cost. Euphoria, on the other hand, may
burst out in the next generation as they revel in a new-found
freedom, explaining away all that has gone before as mistaken,
unreal, or the conspiracy of a few. One such age was the 1920s,
the decade of post-war euphoria variously labelled by its immediate chroniclers 'the Careless Twenties', the 'Roaring
Twenties', 'the Golden Age', even 'the Final Fling'. Like Evelyn
Waugh in his early novels and, later, in *Brideshead Revisited*,
they were describing the life of a small and exclusive group,
those loosely termed as 'in Society'.

Up to the outbreak of the First World War, *The Queen* ran a
regular column called 'The Upper 10,000 At Home and Abroad'
which listed Society events and its participants, the numerical
limit held together by gossip and information exchange. Such a
number had grown from an estimated three to four hundred of

the great families, together with a few wealthy merchants and bankers, of the late eighteenth century. Traditionally, English Society had centred round the Court, and its members were those whose 'wealth, influence and style of living distinguished them from the ranks of landed gentry and enabled them to support a great house and employ it as a centre of social and political influence'.(2)

Throughout the nineteenth century, the system widened in ever expanding social and geographical circles. The English aristocracy have always allowed for such movement, largely owing to the system of primogeniture that has always guaranteed a supply of younger sons ready to enter the Armed Services, the Church or the Bar, and of daughters who, on marriage, moved away from the family seat into another environment. The local landed gentry were not only tied to the aristocracy by marriage and a similar lifestyle, but also linked to the middle class by family ties and common interests in farming. Those common links between the classes, the aristocracy, the landed gentry and the middle class, prevented the formation of an new and angry group, alienated from Society, as was the case in France.

The system was severely tested with the new industrial wealth, except in London where Society has always been more ready to combine new money with the existing élite. Where a function of Society had been to filter the flow of newcomers into its ranks, and thereby maintain its preserve of political power and economic position, in the latter half of the nineteenth century this prerogative was gradually whittled away. Individual achievement was rewarded without reference to Society, as 'political office became elective; professional and civil service appointments were open to competitive examination; the public school became reorganised as a necessary adjunct to middle- and upper-class lifestyle'.(3) Deprived of this control, the more 'theatrical and hedonistic' functions of Society came to the fore, especially that of a 'marriage market', manipulated by women for the benefit of the young.

The First World War, of itself, changed little save to accelerate the tempo of those changes started decades before – such was the speed of that acceleration that it made the difference between evolution and revolution. Those of the older generation who survived the First World War were tired, restless, and no longer certain where they stood. The standards that prevailed before the war, standards of conduct based on people's knowledge of their place and role in life, had largely been diluted. The war had cut across all that they stood for, but had they looked further than the line in their hymnal, 'Change and decay in all around I see',(4) they would have seen, despite the turmoil, evidence of stability. Instead, they merely wanted evidence that underneath it really was the same old world, and hoped for a return to its pre-war order.

In that respect, they were fortunate in that the king, George V, and Queen Mary were both staunchly of 'the old order' and remained so to their dying days. Although at that time monarchy in Europe was decidedly unfashionable, with the defeat of Germany and Austria, revolution in Russia and trouble in the Balkans and Greece, George V stood for stability, and it was his presence that stemmed the stirrings of Bolshevism in Britain. His Court was the very model of decency and sobriety, although many found it dull compared with the raffishness of his father's. Even before the war, he had imposed his simple tastes on his Court, disapproving of what Queen Victoria called 'the society of fashionable and fast people'. The protocol and rituals of Court were rigorously upheld by the Household, equally set in their ways and Victorian in outlook and thinking – Lord Stamfordham, the King's Private Secretary, listening to a fellow peer in a post-war debate in the House of Lords refer to 'Her Majesty's Government', confessed that he 'fancied his mind was, like mine, often wandering back to the Victorian period'.(5) However stiff, formal and retrospective the Court of George V was, it at least revived the Season, the pre-ordained calendar of events.

After the four gruesome years of the First World War, the British of all classes, and especially Society, were determined to enjoy themselves. That first Season after the war seemed like proof that life as they had known it would go on as before, even if their world had changed. Royal garden parties and presentations at Court were revived; there were balls and dances. The first Derby, a record one, was followed by a glorious Ascot. There was polo at the London clubs, yachts were refitted for Cowes Week. Professional cricket and Wimbledon once again attracted the sporting element. Dust covers came off in the lodges on the Scottish and northern English sporting estates and, although the shoots on both sides of the border had suffered during the war, at least the signs were good for the future. Packs of hounds, depleted or disbanded in the war, were reformed, and although the hunting was spectacular by present day standards, the hunting folk complained that it was not as it was before – but that was nothing new, they have been doing that for centuries. The opera and ballet season returned with Dame Nellie Melba at Covent Garden and the Russian Imperial Ballet, released for foreign tours after the Revolution.

The grander members of the aristocracy followed their monarch in reverting to the grandeur of pre-war days, at least as far as taxation, death duties and the lack of servants would allow. The great London houses, like Norfolk House, Devonshire House or Grosvenor House, carried on until they, like Marchmain House in *Brideshead*, were eventually pulled down or redeveloped. In the country, traditionally more resistant to change, estates were broken up, country houses sold or converted into nursing homes and schools. But in those places that survived, the incumbents' lives were scarcely affected.

Compared to pre-war days, little had altered at their preparatory schools either, nor at the other public schools, such as Eton, where traditions often centuries old defied change. Not so at university, especially Oxford, where the style, decadence, even dress, of the richer upper- and middle-class undergraduates exemplified the spirit of the decade, the domination of youth. Theirs was a new-found freedom, which they believed that they had earned by right. Whether aesthetes or athletes, 'arties or hearties', they revelled in their excesses and extravagances. They were a mixed bag – mature students, never ceasing to wonder that they had survived the war, and slightly younger men who had lived under their shadow in the war years. 'Eat, drink and be silly, for yesterday we died'(6) was their watchword, and both groups lived up to it to the full. The admission of women to Oxford in 1920 was further evidence of the changing world, although the dons were more concerned over dropping Greek as a compulsory subject.

The war had upset the balance of the sexes. The spirit of emancipation of the young, particularly young women, was a product of the feminist movement of pre-war years and of the war itself, which not only gave them the vote, but also freed them, upper-class girls at least, from the drudgery of home life and thrust them into what was for them a different and exciting world outside. The modern girl, or 'flapper', had come out and made certain that she was there to stay. Like her male counterpart, she expressed herself in a bizarre appearance and an independent, carefree and abandoned lifestyle. The younger generation of Society, dubbed the 'Bright Young People' by the Press, enlivened the decade with their antics, parties and general lack of inhibitions. Sex was no longer a taboo subject; Dr Marie Stopes's contraception clinics catered for all classes. It was a direct response to the times, a positive reaction to the older generation. There has always been a gap between the generations, but in the 1920s the war had dug an almost impassable ditch. A prime example was the Prince of Wales's relationship with his father, George V. The King loved everything old, the Prince loved everything new, yet the King never made any attempt to sympathise with his aspirations.

But it was the change in the composition of modern Society that was most marked – like everything else, accelerated by the war. 'Really, I don't think they can have known who we were,' complained Lady Stanley when her usual table was taken at her favourite restaurant, to which Lord Berners replied: 'And who were you?'

Lady Stanley should have known better than to have made a remark like that (she was, after all, the daughter of Earl Cadogan), but before the war everyone *knew* who everyone was without having to ask or be told. Nor were they snobs: Jessica Mitford's parents, Lord and Lady Redesdale, would have been

> not so much shocked as blankly uncomprehending, if anyone had accused them of 'being snobbish'. Snobbishness was surely a middle-class attribute, finding expression in an unhealthy desire to rise above one's station, to ease oneself in where one wasn't wanted, and in turn to look down superciliously at those below one in the social scale. My parents would not have dreamed of looking down on anyone; they preferred to look straight ahead, caring not at all if this tended to limit their vision.(8)

Not only was there new money around – the war profiteers had done exceptionally well – but also many titles to dilute the peerage. During the Lloyd George administration more peers were created annually than at any time before or since. Between 1917 and 1921, four marquessates, eight earldoms, twenty-two viscountcies and sixty-four baronies were created. It was no secret that such honours could be bought by the new rich – a practice the Marquess of Salisbury described as 'scandals of the crudest kind . . . the scandals of honours which are said to be put into the market and sold, in order to obtain money for Party funds'.(9) According to the Duke of Northumberland, 'a knighthood cost £10,000, a baronetcy £40,000'.(10)

With a new set of post-war rules, Society was markedly relaxed. Beauty, money, wit, talent, and in some quarters intelligence as well, came to the fore. The days of the great political hostesses died out with the Victorians, with the exception of women like the Marchioness of Londonderry and Viscountess Wimborne. In place of those aristocratic hostesses came a new breed, a special blend of money and intellect, led by such women as Lady Cunard, Lady Colefax and Mrs Laura Corrigan, who vied with each other to hold the most glamorous salons and to patronise the arts. It was a Society where the writers of yesterday mixed with the novelists of tomorrow, to be parodied by the playwrights of their day, such as Noël Coward, a man polished in Croydon to mirror Mayfair. It was a society that embraced the loose Hollywood actress, Tallulah Bankhead, with the same grasp as a duke's daughter, Lady Diana Cooper, who in turn was a stage actress.

For convenience, historians and sociologists have divided up the centuries into descriptive ages: 'the Golden Age', 'the Age of Reason' and so on. The more modern the age, the shorter the period – from one million years of the Pliocene to the six years known as the 'Age of Macmillan'. Historically, each of these periods blends into the next, with no firm dividing line. Not so the 1920s. Although not an exact decade, the period so termed fits neatly from Armistice Day, 11 November 1918, to the day Britain came off the Gold Standard on 21 September 1931. The twenties heralded the new age of change, from the old pre-war order to the new, and it went on changing throughout the decade, as the economic climate altered. After the war, there was an uncontrolled inflationary period, prices soared and fortunes were made. The bubble burst and the slump that began in mid-1920 caused mass unemployment. There was a mild recovery from 1923 until 1926 (the year of the General Strike) but this was followed by the near total collapse accentuated by the Wall Street crash in the United States and a series of financial scandals in the City. With each change in the economic fortunes of the country came a wilder reaction in the mood and lifestyle of Society. The Jazz Age and the dancing craze, which pervaded all classes, were both born out of the first slump.

While the younger generation danced and laughed their way through one economic crisis after another, the majority of the older generation, whose life's work was not to alter their lifestyle whatever their circumstances, believed that bankruptcy was around the corner, whatever their financial position. Although there were all too many cases of real hardship, like war widows living on inadequate pensions, the majority were just marginally less well off – one peer continually reminded his family that they were all about to enter the work-house, despite his estates of over 100,000 acres.

Of the many novelists and chroniclers of Society in the 1920s, Evelyn Waugh is possibly the best known and the most widely read. Although not born into Society, he was accepted for his 'talent to amuse'. He wrote with an outsider's view of the world he craved, portraying it both satirically, as in *Vile Bodies*, and more poignantly in *Brideshead Revisited*. *In Society* charts that rarefied and privileged world.

1

CHILDHOOD

'To see a friend
. . . name of Hawkins'

*W*HEN SEBASTIAN FLYTE ASKED Charles Ryder home from Oxford for the first time, it was not to see Brideshead and its treasures, the famous garden or to meet any of his aristocratic family, but 'to see a friend . . . name of Hawkins'.(1) For Sebastian, Nanny Hawkins and the nursery were the only reasons to visit the house and, in common with generations before and since, he certainly loved her best. 'There was a perpetual quality about one's nanny. She was always there, so dependable, warm and loving. Later, she became my aunt's ladies' maid. She was 'home' – wonderful to come back to for the whole of your life.'(2)

Sebastian, of course, was not a child of the twenties but of the Edwardian era. However, there has always been a timeless quality about nannies and the nursery, and little had altered in their world for fifty years. Most nannies had trained before the Great War, so bridging the gap between the twenties and the Edwardian, even the Victorian, eras. As a rule, the grander the family, the more old-fashioned the nanny and traditional the nursery. The same was true for both country and London, especially where there was a combination of the two, although nursery life obviously differed considerably for country and for town children. Generally, parents were still remote from their children – 'to be seen and not heard' remained the form, one perpetuated by the old-fashioned nanny, who still held considerable power in the nursery. Nanny's power over children, as well as some of the more liberal parents, declined only marginally during the decade, her position secure as her services were thought indispensible. Yet the natural maternal instincts combined with the less regimented life of post-war women, reinforced by the influence of Freud and other thinkers that subliminally filtered into the minds of upper-class parents, did tend to produce increasing conflict between mother and nanny, with the inevitable division of loyalty in the children. One mother in the 1920s had eighteen nannies in four years.

Despite the shortage of other servants, nanny stayed and ruled her domain, the nursery, as she had done for decades past. In grander houses, she was assisted by one or more nursery maids, and in grander houses still, there was a nursery footman as well. The nursery was invariably placed as decently far away from the main body of the house as possible, somewhat in limbo metaphorically between the front stairs (the family) and back stairs (the servants), more often than not on the top floor overlooking the gardens or the front of the house. At Brideshead, 'the dome was false, ... its drum was merely an additional storey full of segmental rooms. Here were the nurseries.'(3) The 'nurseries' were the day nursery, where the children lived, played and ate in the day, and the night nurseries, where they slept with nanny. The furnishings of the day nurseries, like their siting, were always the same – the ubiquitous brass-topped fender in front of the fire, a screen of Victorian cut-outs from magazines, a rocking horse and doll's house. The cupboard housed wooden toys and cardboard games, 'a box of German bricks, made of stone, or stone composite, red, blue-grey and white',(4) children's books, clock-work trains and armies of lead soldiers. Mrs John Dower, sister of the historian G. M. Trevelyan, recalled:

As children, we used to play with lead soldiers which lived in a little cupboard with little drawers, each one housing a regiment. They had been collected by my father [Sir Charles Trevelyan] and his brothers with their pocket money ever since my father was ten, in the 1880s. . . . They took a long time to collect. There are 6,000 [of them].(5)

Nursery routine varied little, being pre-ordained and, in most cases, unalterable. The children were woken at seven-thirty and dressed, often in 'hand-me-downs' as 'it went without saying that well-dressed children had common mothers'.(6) Clothes, when new, came from shops like Rowes, for boys, and 'Wendy', a shop in Bond Street that belonged to Lady Willoughby, for girls. Nanny or the nursery maid would repair their charges' clothes, and sometimes make them as well. Some went as far as to copy those sent down from 'Wendy' on approval before returning them as 'unsuitable'.

Breakfast, prepared in the kitchen by a kitchen maid, was, like most nursery food, inedible. Generally, the better the food in the dining-room, the worse it was in the nursery. The breakfast trays were carried up to the nursery by the 'odd man' (or the nursery footman in those grand houses) and usually consisted of lumpy porridge, an egg dish – generally stone-cold despite the hot-water plates to keep it warm – toast and marmalade.

Having breakfasted, the children were sent down to see their parents in their rooms at nine o'clock, often more as a tradition than a pleasure, on both sides. At Florence Court in Fermanagh, Northern Ireland, the Cole children, plus any cousins or friends who happened to be staying, 'went as far as to keep a silent vigil while their parents, [the Earl and Countess of Enniskillen], ate their breakfast.'(7)

After the ordeal of the first parental meeting, the children of school age were shipped into the schoolroom for lessons with a governess. Whereas a nanny was always from a working-class family, like a groom or tenant farmer, the governess was 'of more genteel birth', and consequently resented by her and the other servants, as well as the children. Invariably, she was a pathetic, lonely figure, straight out of a Brontë novel.

Governesses were not chosen for their academic degrees, still less their common sense. I sometimes wonder if they were ever interviewed before being engaged. They were invariably bitter or very naïve, and once engaged, they were ignored by their employers. It was much more important to ride well or wear clothes well than to show any intelligent interest in things of the mind, though some parents did have their daughters instructed in a foreign language. My Aunt Maud (née Lyttleton), with a wide knowledge of genealogical history – ducal, not the Tolpuddle martyrs, as Nancy Mitford, a self-educated product of the era, says of the Lecherous Lectures – once confessed to my mother her concern of my total ignorance of history and literature. My mother was aghast, but blamed me, not my teachers.(8)

While there must have been some governesses who were adored by their charges, the majority of autobiographies and biographies of the period are consistent in their accounts of unabashed dislike of the wretched governess, and the imaginative methods used to hasten her departure or to make her the butt of their practical jokes. In the Mitford family,

they [governesses] came and left in bewildering succession, and each replacement brought with her a new slant on the sum total of human knowledge.

Miss Whitely taught us to repeat "A-squared-minus-B-squared-equals-A-squared-minus-2AB-plus-B-squared", but she did not stay long enough to explain why that should be so. Boud [Unity] found out that she had a deadly fear of snakes, and left Enid, her pet grass snake, neatly wrapped round the W.C. chain one morning. We breathlessly awaited the result, which was not long in coming. Miss Whitely locked herself in, there was shortly an ear-splitting shriek, followed by a thud. The unconscious woman was ultimately released with the aid of crowbars, and Boud was duly scolded and told to keep Enid in her box thereafter. Miss Whitely was succeeded by Miss Broadmore.(9)

After morning lessons, children generally lunched with their parents and the hapless governess, who, like the children, was usually ignored. If there were guests, governess and children had lunch in the schoolroom together, which was unpopular with staff and children alike. Lunch was followed by a walk or a ride, whatever the weather. The walk was often combined with a nature study lesson with the governess.

Dancing classes were an essential part of growing up. In the country, classes were held in town halls, local hotels or rotated around the houses of the various pupils. There, 'little girls in organdie dresses and cashmere shawls, accompanied by starched nannies, were delivered by their chauffeurs'(10) and taught by some hired teacher to the accompaniment of a pianist. For many, dancing classes were the only contact with their contemporaries, all, of course, from similar, upper-class backgrounds. From the very beginning, children were unaware of the middle classes, but not of the working class. While in the holidays, at weekends or after lessons, upper-class children in the country were encouraged to play with the village children, they never came into contact with middle-class children in case 'they had to be asked back to tea'.

Nursery tea was special, especially in winter when toast could be made on a toasting-fork in front of the fire. Whilst the strict nanny regime forbade butter with jam, cake before bread and butter, and anything but a plain cake unless it was a child's birthday, the more liberal families indulged their children. Children, made tidy in their day clothes, went down to see their parents again for an hour after tea in the drawing-room – the offspring of the very grand reverted to the pre-war tradition of having their children brought in in starched dresses or sailor-suits. Often they just 'sat twiddling their thumbs and then went up again'.(11) The more benevolent parents saw their children before bedtime as well, the mother reading or telling them a story; more often, the parents were 'out gadding by the time their children were in bed.'(12)

Sundays differed in that children accompanied their parents to church, where their father often read the lesson. Frequently, their attendance stemmed from a need to set an example to the staff, tenantry and villagers rather than from any deep-rooted faith in God or the Church of England. To set their children off on the right lines, mothers often read them a chapter of the Bible or a religious story. Some families took Sundays more seriously than others – in the Pakenhams' house,

> entertainment on Sunday presented problems, for tennis was banned and croquet only permitted in the hours be-tween church services, as my mother had a theory that the sound of the balls was audible in church. . . . She also banned Sunday newspapers. . . . Anyone wishing to catch up with world events, Saturday's sports or the song hits that were published weekly with additional verses, was obliged to seek the butler's pantry whither the prohibition did not extend.(13)

A London childhood was generally a more difficult matter for both parents and children. In the country, children were ex-pected to amuse themselves; they had their ponies and their dogs, and it was perfectly safe to walk anywhere. In London it was a choice of having the children cooped up in the nursery or 'milling round the house all day. It was also unsuitable for them to go out on their own, some occupation had to be found for them at every waking moment of the day.'(14) One typical London childhood spent in the Boltons, a particularly pretty square of large houses in South Kensington, is recalled here:

> In the twenties, there were very many fatherless families like ours – in fact my father died of war wounds in 1922. For most of the year, we lived in the Boltons, in a house that my parents had bought, and which remained in the family for fifty years. There were five children, three boys and two

girls. At the top of the house was the large day nursery and two night nurseries – the oldest boys slept downstairs. We had two nannies, one left to get married and she was replaced by the Beauchamps' nanny. There was always a nursery maid who did our clothes, looked after the nursery floor and brought up the food for all meals from the kitchens five floors below. Our cook, Fan, was wonderful and really ran the house, doing *everything*. When we outgrew Nanny and went to day school, we had a sort of governess. She was there when we came home but did not really teach us anything.

My mother was tremendously busy. She wrote hundreds of letters. We had our own special post box outside the house, and letters were collected throughout the day, the last collection being at ten o'clock at night. Even those letters arrived by the first post the next day. Like her contemporaries, she spent much of her time with charities – the family still support one of her charities, the Bishop Creighton House in Fulham. We had an aunt who was a nun in an open order in the East End [of London]. On the same day every year, four rickety old taxis arrived at the house bringing some old ladies, dressed in black in marvellous hats, for a tea-party in the garden. They enjoyed it enormously and they all left with flowers and cakes – my mother was a great gardener.

The great thing about a London childhood was that we had to be kept busy all the time. There was a walk every day. We usually went with Nanny to Kensington Gardens, where she met her friends and we met ours, it was really quite jolly. We all belonged to the Guides or Brownies, where we met the children of our parents' friends. We learned to ride in Rotten Row in Hyde Park on mounts hired from Smith's Stables off Sloane Street. Every day, one or more of us went with an aunt, who also lived in the Boltons, for a drive round Hyde Park in her landau. In those days, most of the tradesmen delivered by horse and cart – the butcher and baker dressed in striped aprons and straw boaters. They were very good to us, giving us rides around the square in the carts. There were also muffin men, with trays of muffins on their heads, ringing their bells and shouting their wares.

We never went to the country at weekends during the school term. On Sundays, we went to the zoo or to some museum in the morning. After lunch, which might have been chicken for the children as a special treat (the 'grown-ups' always had more common fare, roast beef), we went to Sunday school – we followed Canon Woodward wherever he was preaching. His churches were always packed. If we were in London during the holidays, our mother would arrange some form of visit for us – to a livery company in the City, a factory or something of the sort.

Children's parties were very much as today with entertainers or a Punch and Judy show or a visit to a pantomime. We went to dancing classes, there was a place in the Gloucester Road which was quite close, or we went to Madame Vaccani.

What is a particularly vivid memory of the time was the terrible fogs. They were real pea-soupers. If you went out, you felt your way along the railings and had to wear a mask. Men even had to guide the buses along the road.(15)

Apart from Kensington Gardens there were other parks and private gardens to play in like Hamilton Gardens, behind Piccadilly and backing on to Hyde Park, – Thackeray had mentioned them as the 'playground for blue-blooded children'. In the late 1920s, they served as the playground for the young Princess Elizabeth, the Lascelles boys and children of other aristocratic families. They may have been exclusive but they were also dirty, for, in the days before smokeless fuel, the grass and shrubs were covered in soot. '"Don't touch anything, darling; it's so nasty and dirty in this garden."'(16)

Children brought up in the country were encouraged to amuse themselves when not in the schoolroom or closeted with their parents, particularly in the school holidays when they were joined by their 'town' cousins. There was always plenty to do. Some families with a gardening tradition gave their children small plots to cultivate – 'small beds in a line where we planted packets of seeds of flowers and probably a few vegetables which we tended with our own special cut-down gardening tools. We had our own little garden house where we kept everything. It had tables and chairs and a little stove.'(17)

As the majority of landed families spent their lives in the saddle, shooting or on the river bank, it was only natural that their children should follow suit. The usual ponies were kept, and, like the hand-me-down clothes, were passed on from brother to sister or cousin. Hunting was naturally encouraged in hunting families – meets in the school holidays being over-run with children on small ponies. Sons generally took precedence over their sisters – one Leicestershire daughter recalling that 'it seemed only right that I should give up my horse in the holidays so that one of my brothers could hunt. It was something that I never questioned.'(18)

Game-keepers were divided between loyally welcoming the attention of their employers' sons and finding them a 'darn'd nuisance'. For the boys, it took years to be accepted as one of the guns on a full-scale shoot. They began 'by raising Hell with the rooks or an unlucky pheasant in the hedgerows' with a .410 single-barrelled shot gun. The next step was to go out with the guns on a shoot and just watch. At around fourteen, they were allowed to carry an unloaded gun, usually a .20 bore, then go as a walking gun with the beaters until, finally, the great day came when they took their place as one of the guns after a full six years 'apprenticeship'.

Fishing, a comparatively safer and more sedentary sport, allowed children greater freedom. Children whose fathers were keen fishermen were actively encouraged to follow suit. Ian Anstruther, brought up in Scotland, found that 'it was marvellous, the burns were teeming with trout and all you had to do was put a fat worm on a hook and out they came. It was great fun for a small boy.'(19)

Often older, fatherless boys who had outgrown the nursery would have a tutor for the holidays, usually an Oxbridge under-graduate not much older than themselves. They were there to teach 'manly pursuits', rather than give lessons.

Summers in retrospect are always long and sunny. Diana Mosley's recollection of summer at Swinbrook is typical of the time:

Schoolroom life was humdrum, but the holidays were perfect. Tom [her brother] came home, and we dashed about to dancing parties in the Christmas holidays, tennis parties in the summer. We had been brought up to despise games, [field] sport was all my father cared for; golf and cricket were considered beyond the pale. Tennis, however, Tom and I played, though not at all well; we did it because it led to endless parties.(20)

Some families went as far as having their own professional to coach the children and 'give the host a game'.

For the more fortunate children of the larger, social houses, the holidays were

magic. We had literally dozens of cousins and second cousins who all stayed for Christmas and the summer holidays. Christmas was definitely a religious day first (early service and then Matins) and a jolly one second. Each member of the family had a chair with their name pinned onto it in the drawing-room with all their presents piled onto them. They were opened after lunch. That was followed by a mixed hockey match in the afternoon. Then there was a large tea party in the hall with all the staff and farm tenants and estate workers with their families. The children performed a nativity play and we sang a few carols. In the middle of the room was a vast Christmas tree lit by real candles. Four of the gardeners stood by with wet sponges on the end of long bamboos putting out the dangerous candles. Then my uncle handed out presents to everyone, usually what they had asked for. It was all quite wonderful.

The summer holidays were the best. Unlike most of our contemporaries, we were dreadfully spoilt. We had everything – ponies, a swimming pool, fishing, picnics, a cricket pitch.

What was so good for all of us was that we knew all our cousins well from those holidays. When we all grew up and went to dances, there was always somebody we knew which made the whole thing less frightening. I felt sorry for those poor girls stuck in the country who knew nobody.(21)

At some stage in the summer holidays, the more fortunate children were taken to an up-market seaside town like Frinton, Bembridge on the Isle of Wight, or to the Cornish coast, with their nanny, and possibly a nursery maid. Some parents visited their children once or twice during the holiday, when they would 'get into the sea, which I [Mrs Richard Cavendish] should think was the nastiest thing that ever happened to them. They'd come down for about three minutes and then go away again. They'd done their duty'.(23) Often the whole family would go off to the seaside. This typically happy recollection is of holidays spent at Porthpean, on the south coast of Cornwall, throughout the 1920s:

When I was small, six and under, my brother and sister, my parents, our nanny and I went to stay at 'The House' with my grandparents. We moved over to the 'Glen', the next door family house, after my uncle, my father's next brother, married in 1921 and later brought his family to stay too. It was a veritable rabbit warren of rooms which housed a great many relatives – my other grandmother, my aunts and cousins, who usually came to stay; also four servants and visiting nannies, as well as ourselves.

There was only one small bathroom and two lavatories. As it was a real picnic house, no one minded the discomfort.

Travelling from London was a *great* occasion. My father hired a sort of bus, a brake I think it was called, with the seats down the sides. We all piled into this with masses of luggage, parents, children, and servants and drove to Paddington Station to arrive at least one hour before the train was due to leave. There was time to get comics: 'Tiger Tim', 'Rainbow' etc.

My father had reserved three compartments, one for us children and our nanny – Yuja we called her – and the nursery maid, one for my parents and one for the maids.

Our nanny produced two large, white dustsheets and pinned them on to the seats with vast safety pins. In retrospect, I believe it was to prevent us catching 'nits', but we did not, of course, know about such dreadful things. Also, she took our own 'potty' as the train lavatory was much too dirty to use.

The journey was rather dull as far as Exeter, though we took our lunch in a big picnic basket. There was great excitement for us little Pethericks when we crossed the Saltash Bridge into Cornwall as we were half Cornish and felt we belonged.

Arriving at St Austell, we were met by my grandfather's chauffeur. What happened to the maids and luggage I did not know, or consider, but they all duly arrived.

The first thing we did when we got there was to dash down the steps to the beach – gorgeous sea-smells and seaweed, and the call of the gulls. No bathing was allowed the first day after our journey. In the [eight] weeks that followed, the days on the beach were full – sand-castles to build, tin buckets to fill which rusted in the sea-water, rock-pools to explore and paddling in the sea.

We were dressed in white dresses, both girls and boys (when small), and white knickers which were poked into rough and rather scratchy 'paddlers' made of rubber? with elastic round the legs and a bib which came up at the front and tied at the back. We often bathed in long Navy-blue bathing dresses, with buttons on the shoulders. Straw hats were worn – or bonnets for the babies. A cabbage leaf was put inside the hat, on hot days – my father's idea to prevent sunstroke. He was a very kind and gentle person and adored Porthpean. He taught us to catch shimmies [little fish] in the pools, with a stick, string and bent pin, baited with limpets. He also taught us how to find cowrie shells, which I love to collect to this day. He taught us how to row a boat and had a pair of light-weight oars to use in the dinghy. We had to swim the length of the beach, some 250 yards or more, before we were allowed to go out in the boat alone.

Our father's three brothers were our great friends. They

were so funny on picnics, always dressing up and amusing us children. As we grew older, we were taught to catch shrimps. We got to know the best pools, and stalking on the incoming tide was great fun and quite a skill.

Our grandparents seemed rather old, though probably only in their fifties. My grandfather had a yacht with a captain and crew. We were sometimes allowed to go out for the day to fish. My grandmother was a gentle lady but rather nervous. She wore a black hat and a black dress down to the ground.

We sometimes went on picnics to other beaches and got to know the loveliest places in Cornwall which included Land's End and the Lizard. Often we went on blackberry picnics and came back with big baskets full. Another time we went to climb Brown Willy and Rough Tor [two Cornish hills]. We also visited the clay-mines and saw the clay drying process in big sheds. The men had white clothes and white faces!

Those were very happy days, full of activity, and sometimes a quarrel or two but not often. We all got on very happily, and those of us still alive still do.(22)

Not all seaside holidays were remembered with such fondness. Often they were not for the children's benefit at all, but for the parents to entertain their friends and relations. The result, however, was just the same for the children, as the cousins and their friends could go off on their own.

Like members of the Royal Family, the children of grander families migrated to Scotland in August. Such distances were invariably covered by train, at least so far as the children were concerned. Few were as fortunate as Michael Astor, whose father, Lord Astor,

had a deep affection for his children. His concern for them and their health drove him to extraordinary lengths. When, in the 1920s, Lord Astor travelled to Scotland with his family for the summer holidays, he took with him on the train a *cow* and a cowman from the home farm at Cliveden. The cow was milked at Edinburgh and the little Astors nourished without having to drink strange milk. Then the Astors and the train proceeded further north and the cowman and cow went back to Cliveden. Whether the cow and cowman were brought back for the return journey, Michael Astor can not remember . . .(24)

To many upper-class children, Scotland was, of course, home and life was very similar to that south of the border save that it was generally wilder and wetter and it took longer to go anywhere.

While the middle classes, from before the turn of the century onwards, thought it vulgar to have too many children, the aristocracy and coal miners alike assiduously produced large families. Consequently, the upper-class children of the twenties had dozens, in not a few cases over a hundred, cousins and second cousins, creating a vast network of relations to stay with as well as friends for school and later life.

2

SCHOOL

'The Habit of Independence'

*J*N LONDON, WITH ITS DOZENS OF day schools, children left the care of their governesses that much earlier than in the country. While some girls were entirely educated at home by a governess, the majority went away to boarding school or to a London day school. Wherever they went, their education was generally non-existent. Girls went to the schools where their mother's friends sent their daughters, the Montessori method being the most fashionable as it frowned on exams as 'generating an unhealthy spirit of competition'. One such school was

Miss Faunce's establishment in Queen's Gardens, Bayswater, the successor of Miss Wolf's where all the Edwardian young ladies had been educated. Miss Faunce, in spite of being as broad as she was long, managed more or less successfully to be theatrically dignified. She would have called it lady-like. Her constant admonition was not to forget that one was a lady and to infer that this state carried a heavy load in the area of deportment, decorum and grammatical articulation. She had distinct gifts as a teacher of literature and English, in which she was way ahead of her staff, spinsterish ladies of unwieldy shape and bearing whose hearts were not in the business of implanting education in young minds. The more wakeful of the girls led these women off the point of the subject under discussion into personal by-ways which were no more enlivening and the majority of the class slumbered through the daily sessions. The daughters of well-known theatrical families were not subjected to the same exhortations of high standards of dignity as those of Miss Faunce's pupils who did nothing more arduous with their lives than bear titles.(1)

Roedean, the girl's school outside Brighton in the lee of the Downs, celebrated its centenary in 1985. One product of the twenties

wore woollen stockings for lacrosse, blue bags for gym and a hand embroidered djibba for afternoon tea. Maids waited at table and when she was ill a pony and trap took her off to the sanitorium. 'Play up and play the game' was the rule.

Only the top brains went to Oxford. Manners and deportment were more important than academic subjects. The gym mistress had lunch with us and if she caught you sagging you went to deportment classes for a week.

Boys didn't exist for us, or the staff. They were a generation that had lost their boyfriends in the First World War. Instead, we were very good at games, with stick practice before breakfast. At least we started the day not looking as if we'd just got out of bed. When I left school, I was absolutely tongue-tied with men.(2)

After day or boarding school, the majority went off to be finished abroad, Paris and Florence being the most popular.

Boys were sent off to their private (preparatory) schools that much later than today, around nine, having outgrown the schoolroom at home or their day school in London. While there were hundreds of Llanabba Castles (Dr Fagan's school in Waugh's *Decline and Fall*), there were only a few 'Leading Schools on Church and Gargoyle Scolastic Agents' books',(3) among them Summer Fields, Oxford, Ludgrove and Heatherdown. Whatever the school, there was a certain similarity in every boy's experience:

There was that terrible train from Victoria. Everyone was weeping, or trying not to weep, as we clutched our tuck boxes. We were met by a ramshackle old bus and taken to the school – a vast red brick Victorian pile. I believe that it is an open prison now. The school was something straight out of Dickens, Spartan with tepid baths. We were always cold and hungry; we must have been hungry by the way we wolfed our food. There were those interminable games of football and cricket followed by cold baths, and in the summer we swam in a septic swimming pool called 'The Plunge': green slime and full of frogs. We did not know we were unhappy at the time as we did not know any different. There were the usual pederast masters that you get in all private schools. The only sympathetic person about the place was the butler, Mr Walmshurst, who showed the film on Saturday night. I suppose the education was all right as I managed to pass into Eton.(4)

'There is no understanding England of the twenties and thirties without understanding Eton.'(5) During that period, no other single institution, let alone school, played such 'a part in forming the mind and temper, the character and taste of the country'.(6) Eton's sphere of influence was wide (although not altogether approved of), not only in the Cabinet (both sides), the corridors of Whitehall, the City, the Diplomatic Service, ('there is an Old Etonian in every Embassy and every gaol in every country'), as well as in economics and the arts, especially literature; and not least among the majority of land-owning families and the Master of Foxhounds Association. As today, its very name conjured up an image of éliteness and success, quite unlike any other English public school. It was patronised by the sons of the rich, the famous and the aristocratic, or those with like pretensions. Not surprisingly, its pupils 'came out on top because thanks to the prevailing social system they had started there.'(7)

The sense of superiority and éliteness of the Etonians at Sebastian Flyte's epic lunch party (who noticed Charles Ryder with 'a polite lack of curiosity which seemed to say: "We should not dream of being so offensive as to suggest that you never met us before"')(8) was all born out of an ancient and unique system. Practically everything about Eton set it, and its pupils, apart from all other schools (particularly the rash of new public schools of the twenties, like Stowe). Etonians still had a predominantly classical education, well taught, and the tone of the school was classical. Its traditions were as old as its beautiful façades, some dating from the fifteenth century. It was an institution that had enjoyed Royal patronage, not least from the doe-like devotion of George III, and possessed considerable wealth since its founding by Henry VI in 1440. Even the school dress of tail-coats and top hats, the same as worn today, could be seen as a somewhat pretentious and arrogant defiance of the times. Their football, fives and the Wallgame, 'a game of such stunning boredom that nobody plays it or wants to',(9) were, and are, different too. Above all, being so insular, Eton had escaped the high seriousness of Dr Arnold, whose aims and priggish reforms, that spread to many public schools, developed character at the expense of intelligence. Eton simply bred individualists, by treating each of its pupils as an individual, as one Old Etonian found:

From the moment I arrived for my first half [term] at Eton feeling like an inky private school boy, I was treated like a gentleman. I had my own room, whose furnishings I had chosen. I could even forbid entry at will, in theory to my housemaster as well. Even at that age, we were all addressed as gentlemen: 'Gentlemen may wear half-change [a tweed jacket] after twelve', or ironically, 'will the gentleman who removed my umbrella . . .' – all of which is not just a mannered tradition but a pious assumption and a delicate hint that to succeed at Eton it was necessary to be something more than obsessively first in Greek construe [translation] or Keeper of Sixpenny [captain of cricket]. It was necessary to be independent – in the first hectic weeks very necessary.

I have very clear memories of the place: finding my way round a small town, among eleven hundred people, to confusingly named buildings – New Schools were built in the 1870s – with the correct books; being responsible for part of my own food from my own pocket and doing most of my work in my own time: it was a decided and uncompromising lesson we all had to learn in those first weeks. Later I aspired to the Sixth Form where we wore stick-ups [wing-collars] and to Pop [the self-electing Eton Society] where we wore fabulous waistcoats.

When I close my eyes and think of Eton, I can hear the chimes of Lupton's Tower and the seven hundred voices in College Chapel; I can still smell the scent of limes in the Long Walk. Eton not only showed me good manners, but gave me the habit of independence. That is something you never lose, even if you never wear the tie or go back to the Fourth of June.(10)

A typically nostalgic view perhaps, but nevertheless, one generally held, and with good reason; for the 'pious assumption' was, that since the pupils would inevitably succeed in the world together, they might as well become used to clubland mores immediately. Etonians, palindromic gentlemen of 'Note' to the man, have always had an especial penchant for writing memoirs of their schooldays. To enlarge on the above recollection will serve as a general impression of the place at that time.

The rooms so described were uniform and small. Lord Home, a contemporary of the period, recalled that years later he took the 'wife of the President of Pakistan to see a typical boy's room at Eton. She was disbelieving and was sure that it must have been the clothes cupboard.'(11) The furnishings of all the rooms, as Henry Yorke, later better known as the novelist, Henry Green, soon discovered on his arrival, were identical:

> We found a wallpaper of trellised roses, a bed, a writing table and a bookcase over it, both of which could be locked with keys which opened every other boy's table in the house, it was all of a pattern even to the keys, a small grate, a small window (invariably open) and an easy chair with a sort of hard mattress in red material. (The bed folded back against the wall in the daytime.) There must also have been a table to have tea on, I forget, but one's clothes went in drawers which were part of the writing-desk. All the wood was varnished black and had lumps knocked out and names cut in. We could hang pictures on the walls . . .(12)

The pictures were also of a type, mostly sporting prints; the richer boys bought watercolours of Eton done by an old lady, Nora Davison, who painted views of the principal college buildings, all day and every day, whatever the weather.

A boy's room was undisputedly his own territory: even his housemaster had to knock before entering, which he did every night on his house rounds. It was accepted as convention that he should make enough noise to warn any boy of his approach in case he was 'engaged in some illegal activity'. A good housemaster made for a good house, and *vice versa*. He set the tone of his house, which in turn was administered by the head of house and backed up by the Library, a self co-opting body. They had more or less unlimited power over the thirty or so juniors. With a weak housemaster, the Library took over, which made for spoilt and arrogant young men and a place of misery for the boys. Then, beatings were commonplace. One member of the Library was 'thankful that the wretched boy with his head on the table being beaten could not see the obvious delight on the face of his head of house, as he ran across the room, wielding his cane.'(13)

Both bullying and homosexuality also went with houses. On the pretext of finding venereal disease, Ian Fleming's housemaster inspected the whole house 'in a state of nakedness'. Eton has always been considered a hotbed of homosexuality, *le vice anglais*, by outsiders. One school of thought maintained that as

Eton provided a classical education, it was bound to be predominently homosexual, as were the majority of those ancient authors. Cyril Connolly endorsed the idea:

> Platonism was everywhere, popping up in sermons and Sunday questions, in allusions to Neoplatonism, in essays by Dean Inge, at the headmaster's dinner-parties, or in my tutor's pupil-room . . . For there was no doubt that homosexuality formed an ingredient in this ancient wisdom. It was one forbidden tree round which our little Eden dizzily revolved. In a teaching conscious, and somewhat decadently conscious, of beauty, its presence in the classics was taken for granted; it was implicit in Plato's humour and aesthetic. Yet Eton, like all public schools, had no solution for sex . . .(14)

Such was the sexual background of both Sebastian Flyte and Anthony Blanche when they left Eton to go up to Oxford.

At Eton, then as now, it was possible to eat at practically any given moment of the day. Although the food provided differed from house to house, it was generally notoriously bad. When a boy committed suicide during term-time, his housemaster asked the house if anyone could throw any light on the reason why he should take such a step. After a few moments' silence, a small voice piped up, 'Please Sir, could it be anything to do with the food?' Tea was generally the best meal of the day, bought and cooked by the boys and eaten with friends, in their own rooms. It generally took the form of a high tea with fried eggs, sausages, bacon and toast. Sometimes it was grander fare, as when Cyril Connolly was invited to tea with Brian Howard (the prototype of Anthony Blanche in *Brideshead*) to find the table spread with *foie gras* sandwiches and strawberries and cream. Michael Astor remembered a gipsy selling teal, 'suspended from a stick like an onion-seller',(15) undoubtedly poached, for the more adventurous boys' tea. The richer could also order up more elaborate food, such as grouse and pheasant from Rowlands, the officially approved café, but it obviously suffered from its journey through the streets of Eton on its way to the tradesmen's entrance. Uppper Boys could use Tap, a rather gloomy bar where they could drink a maximum of one pint of 'none too inebriating beer or cider' while their juniors gorged themselves on 'strawberry or banana messes and drank iced coffee topped up *à la Viennoise* with cream.'(16) The younger boys also had to cook for their fagmasters.

For the first two weeks of a boy's first half, his only task outside the classroom was to find his way round and discover what Eton is all about. Thereafter, until he reached Upper

School, he was required to 'fag' for the members of the Library of his house – fagging was finally abolished in 1982. At that time one of the privileges of Pop was that they could fag any Lower Boy, regardless of his house. Pop, or to give it its official title, the Eton Society, was the most prestigious body to which any Etonian could aspire. An oligarchy of twenty-four boys and in the main self-electing, it was largely composed of the best games players with a sprinkling of their less athletic friends who were either good company or of 'such intellectual distinction that they impressed even an electorate of such lilies of the field.'(17) To some, the need to be elected to Pop took on an importance which was out of all proportion; in the twenties 'Pop were the rulers of Eton, fawned on by masters and the helpless Sixth Form. Such was their prestige that some boys who failed to get in never recovered; one was rumoured to have procured his sister for the influential members.'(18) Without his elder brother's prowess on the sports field, William Douglas Home was elected to Pop on a popularity vote. He found it a

strange and a dangerous society electorate. It can either give a boy confidence and develop his character, or destroy his character for life. I believe it does the former far more often than the latter. The boys in Pop make no effort to disguise the fact. They wear bow ties and stick-up collars, coloured waistcoats of the fiercest hues and of the strangest materials – of velvet, silk or even crêpe de Chine – sponge-bag trousers, rolled umbrellas, black patent-leather shoes, blue overcoats, spats if they so desire, and most eccentric of all, large seals on the centre of the top and fore and aft (below and above the brim) of their top hats. In other words, they are a sight, but be it said with all honesty, a not unpleasing sight – and they are distinguishable from their non-elect colleagues with as much certainty (with as probably as little justice) as a peacock is distinguished from an owl. They stroll down the High Street at Eton linked arm in arm. They are, in fact, in that small world, gods.(19)

Although the present Lord Longford (then Frank Pakenham) to his disappointment never attained the Pop distinction of having sealing-wax to mark his silk top-hat, he and his brother could at least recognise their own hats, having the largest heads in the school.

How much a boy learned at that time depended entirely on him. The Eton system offered him choice of either the best education in England or to be 'idle beyond belief, and to leave school, after thousands of pounds spent on his education, virtually illiterate.'(20) Eton had the pick of all the top masters of the day, starting with the two headmasters of the decade, Dr Cyril Alington and Claude Elliott. Michael Astor remembered Dr Alington as an impressive figure, 'grey haired and glorious, like some exhibitionist saint who paraded the school in an overcoat made of polar bear skin, and who preached better than any man I have ever heard . . .', and his successor as a dimmer figure, 'whose light I assumed was concealed somewhere under his mortar-board.'(21) They were a brilliant collection of beaks (Eton masters), men such as Andrew Gow who taught Greek and whose highest praise was 'not utterly bad'; the three Headlam brothers – known as Sometimes Angry, Always Angry, and Furious – and the legendary history master, C. H. K. Marten, who taught Princess Elizabeth Constitutional History during the Second World War. There were eccentrics too, like the Reverend C. O. Bevan, who drank a thimbleful of iodine every morning before Early School (a lesson before breakfast, now abandoned), or Jack Upcott, who taught Elizabethan history and who would forgive any boy any misdemeanour who could make him laugh. None, however, was more eccentric than John Christie, the founder of Glyndebourne, who theoretically taught science. Christie took up schoolmastering to satisfy a clause in his father's will to the effect that he had to have a profession in order to inherit. When he had an Early School, he would appear in his dressing-gown, distribute a book on 'Levers', then ring for his butler.

> 'Childs, entertain the young gentlemen while I have my bath.' By the time he had washed, and Childs had provided us with coffee and biscuits, John Christie was ready for a short dissertation on the magic of leverage. He never questioned us, which made us suspect that it was ground which was too dangerous for the teacher. Alas, it was too good to last. Childs' intelligence network had for once become rusty, and Christie over-confident, and the Head Master walked in unannounced. He took in the situation at a glance, and that was the beginning of the end of John Christie's professional career.(22)

Quite apart from the brilliant or eccentric beaks, the good and bad houses, it was that spirit of independence and individuality which Eton fostered that really left its mark on its pupils in later life, whatever their subsequent careers. George Orwell and Lord Home were both products of the same system. Orwell's attitude to Eton was outwardly contemptuous: 'Five years in a lukewarm bath of snobbery'.(23) His assumption of intellectual and moral superiority was unconscious and very Etonian: he was, after all, a tug (a scholar living in College). Lord Home's attitude was one of gratitude. He felt that he had been given 'an introduction to life in a large and various company; a sniff of the value of independence; tolerance; self discipline accepted as infinitely superior to orders; responsibility shouldered lightly; to feel but not to wear one's feelings on one's sleeve; a perception of the fun of living; a recognition that power and authority must be exercised with restraint. All that – while the peace and the beauty and the tradition soothed the soul.'(24)

3

OXFORD

'Et in Arcadia Ego'

$\mathcal{W}$HEN PATRICK BALFOUR WENT up to Oxford in 1922, his father, Lord Kinross, repeated the age-old cliché (just as his father had done thirty years before) that those three years would be the best time of his life. Balfour recalled that he and his clique 'wasted time and money; but we did so with a glorious and reckless abandon. We resented intrusions from the outside world; for we had our own Personalities . . . they *were* Personalities, if only for a short and glamorous reign, within the walls of Oxford itself.'[1] His undergraduate life was that of the rich and clamorous élite of the university, a lifestyle that lasted almost up to the end of the decade, certainly no further. His was the Oxford of Sebastian Flyte and his fellow Etonians, of the 'corrupted' Charles Ryder and the Bullingdon rowdies, of flamboyant aesthetes and eccentric dons, where 'several undergraduates had incomes up to £3,000 a year and so were sought after for their cars and the parties they gave.'[2]

In all outward appearances, 'Oxford, in those days, was still a city of aquatint'.[3] It was a changeless Oxford with its magnificent architecture, its venerable dons, the clocks that struck and chimed all day, all over the city. It was, as ever, a major seat of learning, where the undergraduates who cared had at their disposal the best of everything intellectual, not only from Britain, but from Europe and America as well, and who continued to leave with honours, or at least respectable degrees. The outward forms of the university were the same, it would take more than a World War to change that, but the internal forces, the undergraduates, were somewhat different.

Traditionally, one of the main functions of university was to give undergraduates time to adapt between school and the adult world, to 'sow their wild oats'. Oxford was just such a ground, a place where there were so many other adolescents doing exactly the same thing that they were hardly noticed. At the end of the First World War, both Oxford and Cambridge offered places on a shortened degree course to ex-Servicemen. Those veterans, some of whom had been fighting for four years, went up to Oxford alongside boys straight from school. As a natural reaction to the horrors of the war, and in keeping with the general reflationary mood of the country, they led a fast and riotous life. The ex-Servicemen had come from death and were generally uninterested in learning – the 'eat, drink and be silly, for yesterday we died' syndrome was very much their university code. They set an example of fast living and academic in-difference to their younger brothers, the schoolboy-under-graduates, who were themselves experiencing their first flush of freedom after their emancipation from the rigours of school. The authorities excused the former's behaviour because of who they were and what they had been through, and tolerated the latter's as it was unfair to differentiate between the two. The result was that there was never a 'time in Oxford's history when its under-graduates were so wholly indifferent about their degrees, as they were during those years'.(4) Friends who knew everything about each other, their families, tastes and love affairs, would have thought it indelicate to ask what they were reading. Classical Mods and Greats, Modern History, Law and Theology were still pre-eminent, less so Natural Sciences – 'there was said to be a laboratory somewhere beyond Keble'.(5)

Those who followed after the Service entry had gone down (the 'Brideshead years', for the purposes of this chapter) were greatly influenced by what had gone before, not only in wild and extravagant behaviour, but in social and moral standards as well. There was a certain impatience in that generation, for, being too young to have fought in the war, they felt that they had to make up for lost time which, in their extreme youth, they had not even had time to lose. They followed their academic lead too – six hours' work a week was above average. Evelyn Waugh, who went up to Hertford in 1922, admits to 'total indifference to work. Half the undergraduates were sent to Oxford simply as a place to grow up in. Some concerned themselves with rowing or cricket, some with acting and speech-making, some with pure pleasure.'(6) Lord Weymouth, the present Marquess of Bath, 'went up solely to have a good time with absolutely no intention of learning anything. I had no friends from school [Harrow] so all my friends I made at Oxford.'(7)

There was still little competition for admission, and in some colleges, like Peterhouse and Christ Church, aristocrats were welcomed without an entrance examination. One such under-graduate was the Hon Hugh [Hughie] Lygon, to some extent the model for Sebastian Flyte. Lord Weymouth, who was also at Christ Church, did have to pass an exam when he went up to read agriculture, 'as that was the one subject that allowed you a car, at least legally to have a car.'(8) There were, however, notable exceptions among these aristocratic undergraduates – the Earl of Ava (later Marquess of Dufferin and Ava) won the Brackenbury History Scholarship to Balliol. He, however, 'rested heavily on his oars', falling foul of the Master of Balliol. Ava maintained that 'One must have one's fling', only to be told by the Master, 'Yes, but you've flung too far.'(9)

Another reason that those who used Oxford as a place to be enjoyed for itself are well remembered, as opposed to the many learned scholars or athletes (with the exception of men like Lord Home and G. O. B. Allen on the cricket field), is that their days of extravagances have been recorded in the many auto-biographies and novels of the period.

One of the crop of novelists to come out of the twenties was Henry Yorke, who, in case he was a failure and labelled as such in Society, wrote under the pseudonym of Henry Green, and he typified his set. He went up to Oxford, straight from Eton, in 1922. For one term he was 'the most popular man of his year'(10) and consequently dined out every night. He remembered that he 'was usually put to bed about two in the morning to be called at midday with an orange and soda. Lunch was my breakfast, taken alone and always fried sole and sausages because I thought that by not varying my food I was giving my stomach less to do. I felt extremely ill and every day went alone to the cinema. . . .'(11) When he made it to lunch, or gave a lunch party of his own, he recalled,

> We played at being gentlemen. For the first time we could order lunch to be served in our own rooms by going to the kitchens and talking through the hatch to the chef in his white cap. In the end, I do not know why, the main dish

was always duck. Then we visited the Junior Common Room to choose wine with the head steward and this always turned out to be hock . . . There was no escape from what was thought right for a lunch party, but all the same all through the first year there seemed to be a choice of everything in the world with this extravagance of liberty we found.

Here we fingered long-stemmed glasses and sniffed the wine, holding it up to the light which came through our narrow gothic-ridden windows. We spoke knowingly of vineyards with German names but had to be told when the wine was corked. A lunch party there, if it is to count as a success, should not disperse any earlier than four o'clock. Cigars have to be offered, port and brandy, and one never hears the host saying afterwards of his guests that all went well only he had been unable to get rid of them. For we had leisure and everything was before us.(12)

At Hertford, Evelyn Waugh remembered the 'food abundant and highly decorated. In winter the staple drink was mulled claret followed by port. We drank on till dusk while the "muddied oafs" and "flannelled fools" passed under the windows to and from the river, the track and the playing fields.'(13) In his earlier days, he gave what he called 'offal lunches' of beer and cheese. The term came from a line he heard in a sermon at St Aloysius's (surely the origin of the nomenclature of 'that' bear): 'St Paul says, "All the world is offal."'

Drink played an essential part in their life; many have admitted that they did not draw a sober breath in the whole time that they were up at Oxford. The Marquess of Bath remembered his year as 'a life of hard drinking. Mostly port.' Drinking was essentially a social activity and those who drank alone were to be avoided. Tom Driberg was advised by Evelyn Waugh, already a champion of the bottle, 'most seriously to take to drink. There is nothing like the aesthetic pleasure of being drunk, and if you do it in the right way you can avoid being ill next day. That is the greatest thing Oxford has to teach.'(13) One association that typified the mood of Oxford at that time more than any other was the notorious Hypocrites' Club, so named from the Greek, ἄριστον μὲν ὕδωρ, 'water is best'. There they drank 'as they never drank in pre-war Russia'.(14) It was founded by those who found the formality and the expense of the established dining clubs, such as the Gridiron and Vincent's, too conventional. They set up in a dilapidated house, in a number of bare, uncarpeted rooms above a bicycle shop in St Aldate's, just beyond Christ Church on the way to Folly Bridge. The original members were, for the most part, beer-swilling, aggressive Wykhamists and Rugbians. They preferred darts and shove ha'penny to conversation, although some had a vague artistic or literary taste. However, the food and drink were cheap, and 'nowhere in Oxford could you taste a better omelette or a juicier mixed grill. There was no genteel fear of onions at the Hypocrites'. The smell of their sizzling greeted you on the staircase.'(15) Even the waiters were drunk most of the time – being encouraged to drink by the members, none lasted long and they were sent off to homes to dry out.

By the Michaelmas term of 1921, the original Hypocrites' was occupied 'by a group of wanton Etonians who brought it to speedy dissolution. It then became notorious not only for drunkenness but for flamboyance of dress and manner which was in some cases patently homosexual.'(16) Some of these 'wanton Etonians' were to become known as 'the Oxford Set' or, as they preferred, 'the Aesthetes'. Their number included such luminary figures as Harold Acton, their acknowledged leader and arbiter of taste and style; Robert Byron, their pivot who, from his Eton days, often dressed up as an old woman and looked astonishingly like Queen Victoria; John Sutro, the 'guardian of their youth'; Cyril Connolly, Mark Ogilvy-Grant, Brian Howard, (Billy) Lord Clonmore, Lord Elmley, the President and heir to Earl Beauchamp, the partial model for Lord Marchmain in *Brideshead Revisited*, and Evelyn Waugh (not an Etonian), elected secretary although he did nothing about his appointment. Not surprisingly, with two such disparate groups, the original members resented their intrusion. The new wave talked, long, hard and noisily; no subject was barred so long as it was discussed lightly. They were entirely unselfconscious, never taking themselves seriously. They set out to shock, and succeeded.

The 'pub' atmosphere of beer and dart boards of the originals' club was quickly transformed by the new members. The walls were decorated with murals – those in bad taste, even for the Hypocrites', were expunged by one of the members, a rather surprising don called Sydney Roberts, known as 'Camels and Telegraph' because he was the Reader in Tamil and Teligu. Robert Byron and Oliver Messel (then at the Slade and a frequent visitor from London) painted the more accomplished of the murals. The folk music of the original members was soon replaced by jazz from a wind-up gramophone and, equally in fashion, Victorian drawing-room ballads. Peter Rutter, aged twenty, mourned the loss of his youth while he 'extracted beauty from the most unwilling of pianos, while Mr Robert Byron, looking like some possessed Hungarian Prince, added the gimlet of his voice.'(17)

For its members, the Hypocrites' was too good to last. It was always unpopular with the dons, at least with those who were not members. It was finally closed down, possibly at the insistence of 'Sligger' Urquart of Balliol, who rightly judged it a rival and corrupter of his own sedate group – John Sutro thought that as the club became more and more disorderly, the Proctors closed it because biting went on there! In fact it was just the noise its drunken members made in the street on leaving the club in the early hours of the morning that closed its doors forever.

Lord Elmley gave a dinner at the Spread Eagle at Thame, just thirteen miles east of Oxford, to celebrate his own twenty-first birthday and the demise of the Hypocrites'. The proprietor, a genial man called John Fothergill, remembered the night as

the last, the funeral bake meats, of the just-suppressed-by-the-Proctors club. ... I [Fothergill] have a clear image of David Plunket Greene, 6ft. 9in. high, dressed in white flannel trousers and a thin white vest, and Lord Elmley had a purple dress suit, and as he was 'by the way of coming of age' he supplied the sixty bottles of champagne I set out, 9 in. apart, down the middle of the table, 40 ft. long, that ran close against the wall of the dance room, the rest of which was clear for dancing; and Turville-Petre, who later went to the East to excavate anthropologically and discovered with his umbrella the oldest known skull within a day or two of his arrival. Rudolph Messel, even better looking than Turville-Petre, and quite the vainest, or rather the only vain one of the lot. The Greenidge brothers, pleasantly quite mad. Robert Byron, shrouded in lace trimmings, slept blissfully on the sofa after dinner, pre-visioning Byzantine art, upon which two years afterwards he was considered an authority ... Harold Acton made a speech with his Big Ben-like voice: 'Gentleman, deeeeeer Gentlemen, I wish to propose the toast of "The B . . . a . . . r . . . d . . . y",' a speech full of incredible precosity and rare quotation that would have surprised Aubrey Beardsley. The dancing was terrific. I have an image as of wild goats and animals leaping in the air. It must have been a record party in Oxford's history.(18)

After the club closed, many of the members took over the New Reform Club in the manner that they had infiltrated the original Hypocrites'. Their sheer weight of numbers ensured that they were elected to the major offices of that rather staid club, founded by Lloyd George Liberals for serious political discussion and dignified lunches. Once again, the foundation members were furious with the new rowdy members. One complained that 'There's such a noise that one can not hear oneself speak', at which Evelyn Waugh asked of a very old man lunching in the corner if 'he could hear himself speak?' The man was the only satisfied old member, he was both deaf and dumb. Few of the older members could stomach the behaviour of the ex-Hypocrites and, although they put on an excellent lunch, the cheapest in Oxford (which they ate themselves), it was not long before the New Reform went bankrupt. When the National Liberal officials came down from London to investigate, they found a Conservative and a Communist, and that the rest were a-political with not a Liberal amongst them. By the articles of the Club, Lloyd George was responsible for their debts, which were duly paid out of the Lloyd George Fund.

Another novel and fun institution of the Aesthetes was the Oxford Union Railway Club. The club was founded by John Sutro, who 'had a deeply personal affection for the British railway companies and a feeling for British trains and their affinities that was alternatively lyrical, ethical, aesthetic, practical and patriotic.'[19] He knew great sections of Bradshaw (the railway timetable) by heart. The meetings of the Railway Club were held roughly once a term in the form of a dinner in a private dining-car tacked on to a train. The inaugural expedition to Leicester and back was held on 28 November 1923. Sutro had arranged for a dining-car to be hitched on to the Penzance–Aberdeen train for the party, some sixteen members and guests. They dined, in black tie, on the way out – a splendid meal far removed from the usual railway fare, with great quantities of wine, all served on 'spotless napery' – while they discussed travel since Stephenson's Rocket. At Leicester, their carriage was unhitched while the members drank exotic liqueurs in the station bar for twenty minutes until they caught the train back to Oxford. There was more drinking, toasts, speeches and 'fine oratory' on the return journey, Harold Acton spoke in praise of 'Fantastica' – 'the motion of the train seemed to inspire him to embroider his utterances even more richly than before.'[20] John Sutro, the master of mimicry, spoke rarely using his own voice. He had worked out the itinerary so precisely that they were back in Oxford by midnight. To commemorate the event, Evelyn Waugh presented John Sutro with a cartoon entitled 'The Tragical Death of Mr Will. Huskisson' – whose right leg was severed by a train

train and who subsequently died of the wound. So successful was the Railway Club that it continued until long after they had all come down, ending in 1939. The meetings became more elaborate, usually held on the London to Brighton line, with a chef from a top London restaurant providing the food. A commemorative run was organised in 1963 by Evelyn Waugh, one of its most enthusiastic members, when once again Harold Acton 'seemed to be just as brilliant as ever'.(21)

Although the Aesthetes amused themselves and each other enormously, they were unpopular with the authorities (both for their behaviour and waste of talent) and with their fellow undergraduates – they were generally richer and had a greater capacity for enjoyment. With their self-assured manner, extravagant dress, and in some cases homosexual tendencies, they were seen as marked men by the 'direct ideological descendants of past patriots, winners of wars on the playing fields of Eton, and Old School Tie men'.(22) There were endless accounts of the open warfare between the two opposing groups – the Aesthetes versus the athletes, sometimes called the arties and the hearties. The 'baying for broken glass' was a common sound, a sound well remembered by Henry Yorke who, terrified, hid while groups of hearties rushed about cloisters, 'holloaing' as if they had seen a fox. Another Aesthete returned to his college and joined a group standing round a bonfire, only to find a little later that it was his bed and furniture that had made the blaze. Evelyn Waugh was not exaggerating when, in his prelude to *Decline and Fall*, he described the scene following a Bollinger dinner when the members 'broke up Mr Austen's grand piano, and stamped Lord Rending's cigars into his carpet, and smashed his china, and tore up Mr Partridge's (black) sheets and threw the Matisse into his water jug; Mr Saunders had nothing to break, but they found the manuscript at which he had been working for the Newdigate Prize, and had great fun with that.'(23)

The Aesthetes' rooms seemed fair game for the hearties, being furnished with taste – flowers, real and artificial, screens and pictures, chintz curtains and covers. Their clothes also aroused animosity from the hearties, and many an Aesthete lived in constant fear of attack or, at the very least, a debagging. It did not, however deter them from setting fashions, notably the high-necked jumpers and 'Oxford bags', trousers in fantastic colours and widths. Although Oxford bags are synonymous with the twenties, they had, in fact, been seen before the First World War on a peer up at Christ Church who was Master of the drag-hounds. On hunting days, he attended his morning lectures in a bespoke pair of extra-wide grey-flannel trousers over his riding breeches.

But the hearties did not have it all their own way – during election night in 1923, a crowd of them set on a prominent Aesthete, said to be Harold Acton, dressed in a cloak and evening dress, with a pet monkey on his shoulder, whereupon he felled the leader, a rugger Blue, with a loaded stick before 'evaporating' into the Mitre. The same man returned to his rooms one night to find them being destroyed by some hearties, whereupon he drew out his sword-stick and sliced a thumb off one of the invaders. Likewise, Harold Acton's brother, William, was ribbed by some hearty in Peckwater for wearing a bottle-green double-breasted suit and a crêpe de Chine shirt 'the colour of crushed raspberries'. Acton knocked him out with one blow, then 'with a low titter, flicking his fist with an handkerchief upon the hem of which Callot Soeurs had lavished their most intimate stitching . . . William trotted off to the splendour of his apartments.'(24) It was the same William Acton who went to see a friend in his rooms on the top floor of Tom Quad. 'His friend, not responding to his amorous advances, told him to get out of his rooms. Acton was so drunk that he mistook the open window for the door and fell sixty feet on to the grass below. All that happened was that Willie broke the monocle he always wore and had a displaced kidney, which he probably had before he started!'(25) On another occasion, a dead-drunk hearty wrenched a bottle of Eno's from Henry Yorke's hand and swallowed the contents, thinking it was alcohol. The effect was sudden and splendid – the man frothed and foamed to Yorke's choking laughter.

At that time, Brian Howard (the outrageous Anthony Blanche in *Brideshead*) had a foot in both camps. While delighting in his aesthetic friends, he cultivated a heartier set from within his college, Christ Church, most of whom he had known at Eton. They were titled men, such as Lords Stavordale, Weymouth, Grosvenor and Brocklehurst, and all members of the select hunting and dining club, the Bullingdon. It was said that its members were so grand that they would ask a stranger how many polo ponies he possessed rather than whether he rode. Although Brian Howard, to his intense regret, never attained membership of Bullingdon, he was taken to a dinner. He was toasted by the members: 'Brian Howard – that rare combination, the intellectual and the horseman'. After dinner, members and guests went on the rampage. Howard 'got extremely tipsy, and broke several windows in Peck. 256 panes of glass were smashed altogether – which amounts to £60 at 3s. 9d. each; not counting all the lamps in Peck also.'(26) The Peckwater Quadrangle was a frequent target. After another Bullingdon dinner, the *Oxford*

Chronicle records a similar scene where even window cases were pulled out of the rooms. It concluded that 'The scandal is that conduct which would involve townsmen in severe penalties, publically imposed, is hushed up by college authorities when members of the University are involved, and that, however stern the disciplinary measure taken by the particular college concerned may be, the really effective penalty, public exposure and solid disgrace, is escaped by the culprits.'(27)

Many members of Bullingdon were also Aesthetes. William Acton was a prime example who hunted regularly with the Oxford Drag and the Heythrop. He is remembered for his part in one Christ Church Grind (steeplechase) with Robert Coe going for the same fence: '. . . Coe's steed was white as Pegasus, but lacked his wings, Mr Acton's horse lacked everything. . . . they both achieved their object in the end, with the terrified and involuntary assistance of the combined competitors in the next race.'(28) Brian Howard, who also race-rode and hunted, designed the racing colours for his friends – Lord Weymouth had a particularly stylish set of silks: black and yellow hearts in the form of a cross on yellow and black backgrounds front and back. Other fine race-riders, like Hugh Sidebottom, also came under the Aesthetes' charm. When he broke his collar-bone in a grind, he was looked after by William Acton and his brother, Harold, in William's rooms, who plied him exotic drinks as he lay back on plush sofas and cushions.

The Oxford attitude to sex was adolescent. At that time, the Proctors still had the right to expel beyond the university limits any woman they thought a 'temptation'; there was a late-night train from London, dubbed 'the fornicator', although not much used for that purpose. Oxford was totally male-orientated, and under-graduates were content with their own society. They formed deep friendships during the term, some covertly homosexual, and in-dulged in light flirtations during the vacations.

Cambridge was much the same. John Fothergill recalled two Oxford men arriving at his hotel with a Cambridge Aesthete
of great elegance. The lad descended from the car with his arms outstretched, pushing the air, as it were, with the palms of his lovely hands in an undulating motion . . . At tea, I said to them, 'I have a friend who is thinking of not sending his sons to Oxford because he's been told that the moral tone there is not as good as at Cambridge.' 'It's a lie,' screamed the exquisite, throwing out his lovely hands with passion and indignation. 'Cambridge is *far* worse!'(29)

The women who did go to the grander Oxford parties were mostly the sisters of undergraduates and their friends, and local neighbours such as the Mitford sisters. Daphne Vivian, who later married Lord Weymouth and is now Daphne Fielding, remembers three of her friends who were typical 'camp followers', Olivia Plunket Greene, Elizabeth Ponsonby and Cara Pilkington. 'Elizabeth Ponsonby, a typical product of the age, recklessly charged at life, creating chaos around her. Two white borzois were part of Cara Pilkington's cortège. She was hardly distinguishable from the undergraduates who flocked around her, the only difference in her dress being the thin gold chain that she wore round her ankle.'(30) Their parties were spectacular – at one, there were so many guests that lobster Newburg had to be transported in dust-bins, at another, a small hipbath was used as a punch bowl. There were parties in the country – in barns, where guests dressed as shepherds, or beside the river; there were elaborate fancy-dress parties, where Oliver Messel painted the walls with Landseer-inspired still-life groups of game and shell-fish. Women undergraduates, however, had little part of this excitement.

Undergraduettes lived in virtual purdah, and had little or no contact with their male counterparts. In 1926, the Union went so far as to debate that 'Women's colleges should be levelled to the ground', a motion that was carried by a majority of 223 to 198. Not surprisingly, there was an outcry from the women and a rumour went round that they were lining up on the ramparts of Balliol waiting to scald the inmates with boiling cocoa. *Isis*, the university magazine, even announced that 'the cream of our country's youth will be distracted, if not *enmeshed* [sic]' by female undergraduates. The Principal of Lady Margaret Hall shared these misgivings, for she decreed that none of her undergraduates could go for 'walks, bicycle rides or motor rides' with men (other than her brother) without her permission and that there must be at least two women in the party.

Another feature of Oxford was the succession of splendid practical jokes. One of the cleverest was a lecture given by that 'well-known German psychologist, Dr Emil Busch', alias an undergraduate called George Edinger. The 'visitor' from the University of Frankfurt addressed a large audience of distinguished professors and eminent psychologists from London in the Grand Jury Room in the Town Hall. The 'Doctor's' speech, made in halting English, was a brilliant parody of the jargon that psychologists use, but totally without meaning. The audience was deeply impressed by the lecture and declared that it had given them much food for speculation. They were, however, magnanimous in their treatment of the perpetrators when the hoax was revealed.

Oxford has been described as a place of moods, moods that work in five-year phases. The second half of the decade, the period between the General Strike and the depression, was also 'seized with hectic gaiety. There was a feeling of *après moi le déluge*'.(31) It was still a time when freshmen were advised 'never to go on playing bridge after four a.m. or you will be late for your morning golf', or, as for the Union, 'the Union has two billiard tables and no other feature of importance.'(32) Theirs was a different form of 'hectic gaiety' to their predecessors'. They looked to London for their lead and their amusement. Rich Americans arrived, flinging their money and their international manners around. Cocktails were substituted for Amontillado; London West Enders invaded their parties, bringing with them a night-club atmosphere. Whatever the differences between the two periods, those who were there at the time enjoyed themselves. But, just as their predecessors scoffed at their pastiche society, they were to do the same to the thirties' undergraduates' life, for exactly the same reasons.

4

THE LONDON SEASON

'To be Put up for Auction and to Find no Takers'

*T*HERE ARE ARGUMENTS FOR not having a Court,' wrote Walter Bagehot, 'and there are arguments for having a splendid Court, but there are no arguments for having a mean Court.'(1) This George V accepted, although, given the choice, he would have preferred the first option and to live a quiet, modest life in the country with his wife, Queen Mary, and his family surrounded by country people. But he knew better than anyone else what was expected of him in his position as King Emperor. Although he did not care for the high ritual, the entertaining, the ceremonial duties and the pageantry that went with his exalted office, he carried it with aplomb. He had a great sense of occasion and that, combined with his steadfast belief in his inherited role in life and his critical eye for every detail of tradition, *tenue* and etiquette, made for a grand, but somewhat starchy, Court. His increased income from the Duchy of Lancaster and the falling cost of living, together with various Household economies, at least meant that he had the money to have a spectacular Court.

The King had already set the stamp on his Court in the four years before the war, a somewhat dull and sober one by comparison to the racy Court of his father Edward VII. The four years of wartime austerity, with plain food and no alcohol, even with meals, and no official entertainment, was symbolically ended when the seals on the cellar doors at Buckingham Palace were broken on Armistice Night. It was not long after that, late December 1918, when the Court was revived with all its pre-war splendour with the State Visit of the United States President, Woodrow Wilson.

The post-war standard of entertainment set for President Wilson continued throughout the decade. George V received many of the extant crowned heads of Europe – as the grandson of both the Grandmother of Europe (Queen Victoria) and, through his mother, Queen Alexandra, the Grandfather (Christian IX) too, he was closely related to all of them. In 1921, the highlight of the State Visit of the King and Queen of the Belgians was the Court ball at Buckingham Palace, where it seemed that the French Court of Louis XIV had been revived when the King and Queen danced a *quadrille* with their royal guests. A dancing master had been engaged the week before to rehearse the Dukes of Northumberland and Abercorn for their parts in the dance. The Court ball during the State Visit of the King and Queen of Rumania was no less grand: '. . . the Foreign Office people and the courtiers were in white and green and gold. At about ten, the royalties entered and bowed to the Corps Diplomatique, whose bench is on the right of the throne.'[2] Queen Marie, who had lost her looks, appeared 'ridiculous in a sea-green foam of crêpe de Chine saut-de-lit with goldfish she had painted on [it] herself. Her double chins were kept in place by strands of pearls attached to an exotic head-dress. She was every inch une reine . . . de comédie! The ball reminded me of an engraving of the Congress of Vienna, and was not much more animated.'[3]

Besides the Court balls for visiting royalty and heads of state, there were other balls to mark the more important Royal occasions, a birthday, a coming of age of one of the Princes or Princess Mary, or a wedding. To those 'at Court' they were 'rather fun. While the Royal Family consorted with the Household and their friends, you could see all your friends and relations in really rather grand surroundings. Everyone you knew was there. It was a great show, as good as a circus.'[4] The dress, for both men and women, was part of the grand occasion. Invariably, the women had a special evening-dress made for each occasion (a careful note was made of what was worn in the society papers, *The Tatler* and *The Sketch*, hence the new dress) and showed off as much of their jewellery as could reasonably be worn. The jewellery would include a tiara, brooches, pearl chokers and/or a necklace, handfuls of rings and any orders and medals they were entitled to wear. At a magnificent ball at Petworth House for Melissa Wyndham-Quinn, the European guests all agreed that nothing on the Continent could rival the English jewellery. The men who were not in full dress uniform like the King and his sons, wore Court dress of a black velvet cut-away coat and waistcoat with silver or steel buttons, velvet knee-breeches, black silk stockings, a lace *jabot*, all worn with a cocked hat and sword. Those who knew wore black cotton stockings under silk ones (without them, pink, hairy legs showed through), with black pumps. Before the men danced, they removed their swords, and put them in a pile; as they were generally hired from the same shop, it did not matter if they were muddled up. So stringent were the rules of dress that no one at Court would have thought of deviating from the accepted form. The one exception was the American Ambassador, Brigadier-General Charles G. Dawes, who steadfastly refused to wear knee-breeches – even the compromise offered by the Prince of Wales, that he should leave his Embassy in trousers and change into breeches at the Palace, was refused. All waited for his début at a Court ball, which was recalled by the Prince of Wales as

> an impressive spectacle, this stately procession of ambassadors, ministers, councillors, secretaries, and attachés of embassies in Court dress or uniform, with their wives with trains and feathers, the men making their bows before the Queen, the women their curtsies. But all eyes were straining for the first glimpse of the American Ambassador. Fortunately we did not have long to wait before he appeared in the line. At a glance, it was obvious he had won the day; his trousers flowed unbrokenly to his shoes. My mother [Queen Mary] must have looked glacial.(5)

Not only had the American Ambassador won the day, evening dress became acceptable at Court thereafter.

For a Court ball, guests usually dined at home and arrived at the Palace at around ten o'clock. At the side of the Ball Room was a raised dais for the King and Queen, and their family, and anyone they cared to invite for conversation. Opposite them was the orchestra. For one ball, the Prince of Wales substituted Ambrose's band from the Embassy Club for the orchestra, which was barely acceptable to his parents, but when a cabaret dancer came on singing 'You're my baby' it was too much and she was hastily silenced. Those who were not dancing could sit out on little gilt chairs with red cushions in one of the raised tiers around the room. Some had their own special 'enclosures', such as duchesses, who sat to the right of the the Royal dais, or the Diplomatic Corps to the left. Guests could also wander around the ground floor of the Palace or go in for breakfast in the Ball Supper Room. As at most large affairs at Buckingham Palace, the food was unappetising but the drink, invariably vintage champagne, was plentiful and excellent. 'Carriages', in some cases literally, was at two o'clock. As balls, they generally 'suffered by being organised by a committee (the Lord Chamberlain's office) rather than by the hostess. After all, she was just as much a guest there as everyone else although she was supposed to be the hostess.'(6)

Just as the Court returned to its pre-war glory at the beginning of the decade, so the dust-sheets came off in the great London houses, which opened up with all their pre-war splendour. The ballrooms were converted back from makeshift hospital wards, and what entertaining could be managed, with the shortage of servants, was revived as if 'The Great Interruption' had never happened. The houses were vast, even by the standards of the day. Every noble family of note had a London house and most had managed to keep them, at least until shortly after the war. They were immensely grand, each with a particular feature – the gardens of Devonshire House and Landsdowne House together stretched from Piccadilly to Berkeley Square; Crewe House, off Curzon Street, had a particularly fine ballroom; Spencer House and Bridgewater House, overlooking Green Park, both had magnificent furniture. Park Lane, overlooking Hyde Park, had its share of grand houses too: Brook House, left to Lady Louis Mountbatten by her grandfather, Sir Ernest Cassel (the marbled hall was known as the Giant's Lavatory); Dudley House, above the newer Grosvenor House, home of the Duke of Westminster; Dorchester House, half-way down, with Londonderry House, the site of the present Intercontinental Hotel, at the very bottom. Most were still lived in by the family as proper London houses, just like Marchmain House in *Brideshead*, but some were let, as Lansdowne House was to Gordon Selfridge in 1924. Some remained unoccupied through eccentricity. The eleventh Duke of Bedford maintained two houses in Belgrave Square and kept both fully staffed, but only stayed there twice a year when he visited the Zoological Society. As private houses, their days were numbered. Many were converted into offices or pulled down and redeveloped into mansion blocks or hotels, like Grosvenor House and Dorchester House. Today, most are only a memory although some of the rooms are preserved and arranged like 'peep-shows' in the Victoria and Albert Museum.

Like the houses in their heyday, with their marbled halls, wide staircases and gilded salons, the balls were splendid affairs. The Prince of Wales picked out 1921 as one of the gayest years of the decade. That spring, against a background of the coal strike and the slump,

> I went to parties at many of these fine houses, where formal dinners were still served on gold and silver plates by footmen in the family livery with knee breeches, white stockings, buckled shoes, and powdered hair. One of the most striking of these parties was given by Lady Wimborne at Wimborne House, in Arlington Street, where several hundred guests, including King Alfonso XIII of Spain, danced under the romantic light shed by thousands of candles in massive bronze *doré* chandeliers.(7)

Despite the appalling losses of the war, that nebulous milieu known as London Society carried on expanding as fast as ever. It was, however, still exclusive and difficult for an outsider to enter, but once the *nouveaux* were in, they stayed in, and were then completely assimilated unless they committed some fearful social solecism. Beverley Nichols went cold every time he remembered attending his first grand ball in London, given by the Duchess of Marlborough at her house in Carlton House Terrace. He arrived by a scruffy taxi in the rain exactly at the appointed time and rang the bell:

> Long pause. Ring bell again. Have I got the wrong date? Door swings open revealing major-domo [sic], who registers surprise. Alarming vista through doorway. Footmen in the Marlborough scarlet livery scurrying through the hall to take up their positions.
>
> The doors of the drawing-room are flung open, revealing all the Marlborough grandeur, the sort of furniture that a Hollywood producer would hire for a super-de-luxe production. And in the room, only women. I had arrived so early that dinner was still in progress. The men were finishing their port in the dining room. They had not joined the ladies.
>
> The voice of the major-domo. 'Mr Beverley Nichols.' A flurried duchess advancing to meet me. Various other women getting up. They were so festooned with jewels and ribbons that they looked like Christmas trees in a high wind. Lunatic fragments of dialogue. Nobody knew who I was though I muttered something about Ivor [Lord Ivor Churchill, with whom he had been up at Oxford], gave the duchess some clue. (Ivor, as it happened, was ill.) Then the

men began to trickle in. Beribboned, clanking with medals. Stopping short when they saw me. Who was this person?

I was on the rack for about an hour. At ten o'clock the first guests began to trickle in, the guests who knew the social ropes, who were aware that one did not arrive on time for a duchess's dance.(8)

Nichols was the first to leave, to the sounds of music and the footmen serving champagne.

For those families who were not at Court or in the upper echelons of Society, the resumption of levees, presentations and garden parties, and the renewed Royal presence on other occasions during the Season, were a substitute for the Court balls and banquets and aristocratic parties. In March 1920, the King held his first post-war levee – the traditional assembly where 'loyal [male] subjects were given access to their Sovereign'. It was obligatory for certain men to be presented, such as those with a new commission or promotion in the Services, those in the Foreign Office going abroad, anyone wishing to be asked to a Court ball or indeed anyone else who merely 'wished to pay his respects to his Majesty'. They were generally colourful affairs with Servicemen in full dress uniform – after that first levee, the King noted in his diary that it was 'refreshing to see the old full dress uniform again' after the drab khaki of the war. Those without uniform wore Court dress. Levees were held at noon at St James's Palace, the presentee and his presenter arriving together. After mounting the stairs flanked by Life Guardsmen in red tunics, burnished breast-plates, white breeches and mirror-polished black boots, they entered one of many rooms for an 'interminable wait'. Eventually, they were ushered down a long gallery, lined with Yeomen of the Guard, into an ante-room. From there, they entered the Throne Room in groups of three. The King stood on a dais beneath a canopy, surrounded by members of the Diplomatic Corps. As the presentees' names were read out, they passed in front of the King, bowed from the neck (a 'Coburg bow' introduced by Prince Albert), then left – the whole performance taking less than a minute. Chips Channon, the Chicago-born socialite, recorded in his diary a typical levee that he had 'engineered' for himself in June 1923:

It is a gorgeous male sight a levee . . . much preening and red and plumes and pomp and tightly fitting tunics and splendid English faces. We were in a queue for over an hour. Freddie Anstruther was next to me dressed as the hereditary Grand Carver of Scotland. Suddenly I heard Lord Cromer call out 'Mr Channon to be presented'. I advanced a few paces with as much dignity as possible and, in front of me, on a dais surrounded by the Court and the Diplomatic Corps, was the King. He seemed to have something oriental about him, something almost of a Siamese potentate, and I bowed very low. He dropped his head, as if to grunt, and I backed two paces, and then turned and walked away.(9)

It was generally 'considered bad form to hang around the Palace'(10) and, apart from those who absolutely had to attend, levees were for those 'on the make'. The old aristocracy thought the Royal Family somewhat dowdy and considered it very 'non-U' to be excited about them or even to take an interest in them.

The female equivalent of a levee, the attendance of an Evening Court, was a far more important event for all concerned – except for the Royal Family who had to sit, or stand, through the five presentations a year, held in the early evening throughout June. The presentation marked a young girl's entry into Society – subsequently presentations were made when she married or her husband succeeded to some title. There were strict rules as to who could be presented. Traditionally they were the wives and daughters of the aristocracy, Government ministers, Members of Parliament, the gentry, professionals and Servicemen, even merchant bankers and stockbrokers. Trade, unless it was 'commerce on a large scale', was barred, as was 'the acting profession'. The worst disqualification of all was to be divorced, so much so that if a divorcee tried to be presented, her presentation was 'cancelled' by a notice in the *London Gazette*.

The presentation was made by a woman who had herself been presented, usually the girl's mother or the bride's mother-in-law, though a close relation or friend would do. It was not uncommon for an aristocratic but impecunious woman to present a girl at Court and bring her out into Society for a 'substantial fee' if her parents were ineligible on the social scale. As the presenter was personally responsible for the girl, she was advised to take 'the greatest care . . . in presenting anyone whose position and antecedents are not thoroughly known'.(17)

The first Court after the war was held on 10 June 1921, after a gap of over seven years. Lady Airlie, the Queen's lifelong friend and lady-in-waiting, remembered that occasion where the débutantes were, 'a heterogeneous crowd of all ages, some straight out of the schoolroom, others weather-beaten from years of driving ambulances in France.'(12) Thereafter, they were just as heterogeneous but without the ambulance drivers. Lord Sandhurst wrote of the occasion in his diary, '. . . no trains or feathers; this enables many more to attend, though, of course, the dignity of the show was wanting. The days of "dignity" are vanishing and I lament it.'(13)

Style and fashions had changed, new peerages and ex-officers from the war had widened the 'social net' of those eligible to be presented. The Ceremonial Department went so far as to publish guide-lines for what was acceptable. The Lord Chamberlain decreed that, in the interest of economy, a train was no longer obligatory, although, after the first Court, all returned to the old style of dress. Young débutantes all wore Court dress, although 'women's trains were shorter than at Edwardian Courts, where they had measured three yards, making two on the ground. Now they were just eighteen inches on the ground and head-dress plumes [three white ostrich feathers] were worn just a little bit lower.'(14) Carrying a bouquet was left to the individual. Dressmakers were back in full swing, whether the smart London salons of the established names such as Madame Lucille (Lady Duff Gordon, sister of the novelist Eleanor Glyn), Fiffirella, Reville and Rossiter, or some local dressmaker in the country. The grander salons announced what their clients wore in *The Times*. For the girls, particularly those aristocratic daughters from the country, it was a 'splendid way to get a new dress, in fact two, as the train could be made up into something as well.'

For the young débutantes, hours were spent practising their curtsies, either to their families or, for the *nouveaux*, at special classes. Some practised with a 'table-cloth how to curtsy without getting entangled in a train, and to move off crab-wise so as neither to turn your back on the royal couple nor fall flat on the carpet. If you rose with your weight on the wrong foot you could do just that.'(15)

On the afternoon of the appointed day, the girl and her presenter would arrive in the Mall in their car, with a chauffeur and footman, if they had one. It was considered poor form to drive round Belgravia and Westminster, jockeying for position to be first in the queue in the Mall – those who knew the form would 'arrive as late as possible so that they could go straight into the Presence Chamber and not wait in an ante-room.'(16) Those in the Mall waited under the gaze of the crowds who had come to gape at the spectacle, some suffering the Cockney taunts of the East Enders – 'Look, 'ere's a bloomin' canary' they shouted to one girl all in yellow – and the flash of cameras of the Society Press. At the appointed minute, the cavalcade moved down to Buckingham Palace.

Once inside the Palace, the scene was reminiscent of a very grand cattle market. Débutantes and their presenters were ushered across the Great Hall and up the Grand Staircase into a salon. When that room was full, the Gentleman-at-Arms closed it with a light barrier and they waited, seated on gilt chairs. When announced, they trooped through to the Picture Gallery where two officials let down the débutante's train, then crossed to the door of the Presence Chamber where she handed over her card to an official who gave it to the Lord Chamberlain. When her name was called, she walked towards the King and Queen, he resplendant in a Brigade of Guards uniform with sash and orders, she regal and heavily bejewelled. Other members of the Royal Family stood behind or sat beside them, generally looking bored – the Princes in uniform, the female members of the Royal Family in long dresses. One 1925 débutante remembered the fashions for her presentation as 'ridiculous, very short skirts and a long train. When I drew level with Princess Patricia [daughter of the Duke of Connaught] one of the older members of the Royal Family primly wrapped her train over her knees.'(17) The members of the Diplomatic Corps, in their fine uniforms, stood to the side of them.

The débutante dropped a low curtsy to the King, who usually looked straight through the girl, she then took two paces to the right, curtsied to the Queen, who gave a 'kindly smile' or a vacant stare depending on her mood, and then left by a side door. From beginning to end, the presentation took under a minute.

That, at least, was how it was supposed to have happened. 'Every Court was followed by tales of preceding crisis, spots appearing on previously clear complexions, blinding headaches smiting the healthiest, nightmare disasters disrupting Court apparel.'(18) One woman was stripped to the waist when her chiffon dress was ripped by the weight of her medals and orders; one débutante was so nervous that the Lord Chamberlain could not read her name card as she had chewed it to illegibility; another was violently sick in the Picture Gallery, the situation being saved by an equerry who lent the girl his silk (top) hat. One 'over-petted child of doting parents, had gone through at the run, hardly pausing to give two skips as she passed the King and Queen'.(19)

A presentation for members of the Household and their relations, the wives and daughters of the Diplomatic Corps and Cabinet Ministers was far more civilised. They arrived first, often by brougham, and went into the Palace through a side entrance. They went straight into the Presence Chamber, and, after their presentation, watched the rest of the proceedings from raised daises around the room. They then went into the Ball Supper Room for dinner.

That livelong moment of a débutante's presentation was the prelude for her 'coming out'. For girls, especially those who were brought up in the country by supposedly impecunious aristocratic parents, it was the turning point of their emancipation, the division between the schoolroom and adult life. The grander the family, the less the provision that was made by the mother to prepare her daughter for that 'outside world'. The débutantes of the 1920s were the daughters of Victorian mothers, themselves brought up and brought out at the end of the nineteenth century. The pace and style of their era, which of course included the London Season, was set by the Prince of Wales, not by Queen Victoria. Consequently, the Season was remembered as an essential part of their life, and thus an essential requirement, whatever the cost, for their daughters. In retrospect, most débutantes were not greatly enamoured of the Season, except for the new-found freedom it brought. Some came out many times, until they married or became too old. However, the mothers and married sisters invariably enjoyed themselves, a London Season making a welcome change from a life buried in the country.

The grander families naturally had their own London houses from which to bring out their daughters or the more fortunate of their nieces or friends' daughters. Others borrowed or rented houses for the Season – Lord Vivian, who continually lived under the threat of financial ruin, still managed to take a house at 'the rent of fifteen guineas a week, and in May 1922 we [his daughter and her step-mother] moved into 5 Clarendon Place, with a staff of cook, kitchenmaid, housemaid and footman'[20] to bring his daughter, Daphne, out. Lady Pansy Lamb, *née* Pakenham, remembered her in a letter to Evelyn Waugh '. . . you can not make me nostalgic about the world I knew in the 1920s. And yet it was the same world you [Evelyn Waugh] describe, or at any rate impinged on it. I was a débutante in 1922, though neither smart nor rich I went to three dances in historic houses, Norfolk House, Dorchester House, Grosvenor House, & may have seen Julia Flyte. Yet, even in retrospect, it all seems very dull. Most of the girls were drab & dowdy, & the men even more so. The only glamourous girl I remember was Daphne Vivian . . . nobody brilliant, beautiful, rich & the owner of a wonderful home, though some were one or the other.'[21] The Redesdales' house in Rutland Gate in Kensington was only used when a Mitford daughter came out, the rest of the time it was let to others for the Season.

Although no two Seasons were exactly the same throughout the decade, the format was at least similar. The decade began with débutantes being heavily chaperoned at dances – even those girls who had driven lorries or been nurses during the war – as mothers and aunts tried determinedly to restore pre-war Society. Gradually their hold weakened (chaperones at dances had virtually disappeared by 1924), and the morals of the unmarried girls began to 'slip' until 'the permissiveness of the First War returned by the early thirties'.(22) Sex was never discussed, although even up to the Second World War, girls were continually warned by their parents of the dangers of the white slave trade – the threat of Mrs Beste-Chetwynde and her agents in Evelyn Waugh's *Decline and Fall* was to be believed. No girl was supposed to be safe in the street – 'we were seriously warned not to help an old woman across the road; she'd jab a hypodermic needle into one for sure and accomplices would carry away your body. Also 25% of the taxis in London were in the trade and were especially made with no handles on the inside!'(23)

The supposed high-spot for a girl's Season was her own dance. Society was conducted on a 'chop for chop basis' (then called cutlet for cutlet), so it was important to ask those who were known to have good dances so as to receive an invitation in return. There were grand dances given in the great London houses, ostensibly for a débutante daughter or near relation, but the majority were held in the large, terraced houses within the nucleus of Mayfair, Belgravia and Kensington. Each dance was preceded by a succession of dinner parties, given by various of the other mothers. As the guests arrived for dinner, they took the card with their name which told them who they were taking, or being taken by, into dinner. Loelia Ponsonby, later Duchess of Westminster and now Lady Lindsay, remembered that 'a girl generally had to wait to know her fate till she saw an arm crooked in her direction, but sometimes her partner muttered beforehand, "I believe I am to take you in" – being English he never said it with much appearance of pleasure.'(24) The host led the procession of guests into the dining-room, the rear being brought up by the hostess. Although rather formal, it did at least ensure that everyone entered the dining-room without fuss. The food was as good as the cook could possibly provide and the only alcohol, champagne, came with dinner.

Men were always in short supply, particularly just after the war. Hostesses insisted on even numbers at dinner, consequently virtually any man with a white tie would do, regardless of his appeal. Two of the most common sentences of the season were, 'We don't want any more girls' and 'Could you possibly beat up another man from *anywhere*?'(25) John Beaver in Evelyn Waugh's *A Handful of Dust* was the archetypal man who frequented the twenties débutante scene. Once the man was 'in', his name appeared on any number of lists that circulated round the hostesses, and he remained there until he married, unless he behaved so badly or was so constantly drunk that it was noticed. Obviously, they cannot all have been that bad, but many a testimony to their awfulness survives: Daphne Vivian wrote in her diary, 'Disappointed in the London young men – rather a spotty, weedy crew.'[26] Lady Mary Clive, *née* Pakenham, went further:

The first time that I pushed my way into a London ballroom I was so horrified that I could scarcely believe my eyes. I looked again, hoping they were deceiving me, but alas! they were not. I looked near at hand. Dreadful! I looked to the other end of the room. Ghastly! How was it possible for mortal men to be so *ugly*?

To my disappointed eyes, they seemed practically deformed. Some were without chins. Some had no foreheads. Hardly any of them had backs to their heads.

It was really their heads rather than their actual faces. Some had heads like cucumbers. Some had heads like pears. Some had heads like turnips. None of them seemed to have heads like heads. I realised in a flash what a splendid fashion periwigs were and how right the Guards are to wear bearskins – if only they had put them on at dances.

And then their colouring. There seemed to be no alternatives but all-over yellow or all-over beetroot, except for the ones who had blue chins. And they were such odd sizes. Little peek-a-boo faces on top of hop-poles and huge harvest moons peering out at your elbow.[27]

Once at the dance, the nightmare began. The typical London houses were not designed for dances, nor, for that matter, for comfortable living. Both suffered from the same drawback, the stairs, which for dances were permanently jammed. The houses generally followed the same pattern, with a drawing-room and a back drawing-room divided by double doors on the first floor. For parties, the doors were opened to make an L-shaped room. The balcony, beyond the open French windows, generally covered in red felt against the grime, was a welcome retreat from the suffocating heat in the room. Although furniture had been removed, the room was made smaller by dozens of small, gilt chairs lining the walls, occupied by the mothers and other chaperones.

This breed of women, generally known as 'the dancing mothers', were 'either very fat or very thin, covered with unclean jewellery and [when not in fashion] showing a good deal of décolletage'.(28) Often without their husbands, they were content to gossip and comment on the proceedings. In the early years of the decade, the girls had cards, printed with the numbers of the dances, which could be booked by the men beforehand. Each dance lasted about twenty minutes, which meant that the wretched girls who had no partners felt the pity of everyone in the room as they stood in a huddle in the doorway, waiting for the next dance, or hoping to pick up a latecomer. Lady Mary Clive found that you tried 'to keep an expression of enjoyment on your face and not to look like a Circassian in the slave market that no one has bid for. It was bad enough to be put up for auction, but to be put up for auction and to find no takers . . .'(28) The alternative was to hide in the 'ladies' cloakroom between the racks of coats and endure the contemptuous glances of the maids.'(30)

For those who were dancing, it was only marginally better. Contemporaries remember the rooms brightly lit, intensely hot in the smaller houses, the floor crowded with shuffling couples. It was thought ungentlemanly for the man to be able to dance well, that being 'left to the lower orders, gigolos and foreigners'.(31) Taking no pleasure in dancing, partners talked as they danced, usually about the floor and the band, which was always the same. Most girls with any pretence of intelligence kept it dark and fell in with the general conversation, or lack of it. Racing was a good topic, usually the only topic.

At around midnight, the luckier girls were taken down to supper in the dining-room by some man – the chaperones were usually there before them. There, they waited in a queue for the food, which was invariably identical to that served at every other dance. The usual fare was chicken and/or salmon, coated in a white sauce, and strawberries, often served on the same plate. Occasionally the hostess would provide something more exotic like quails, plovers' eggs, baby poussin, even caviar. Like the food, the band and the floor, even the plates and glasses were identical, having being hired from the same firm of caterers. As there was such a crush, such respite from the dance floor was short-lived, and the girl then fought her way back upstairs, where she stayed, dancing or not, until it was time to go home. The best thing that could happen to her was to escape to a night-club, but such behaviour was naturally frowned upon by the hostess as she lost a useful man. When the dances became more relaxed, it was easier to slip away or to take in several dances in a night, whether invited or not.

By the end of the decade, gate-crashing was quite the norm. The young found it 'divinely amusing' to tour Mayfair and drop into any house where there was a party. Some went so far as to forge invitations to dances, copying those of their friends who had been invited, while others just tagged along with their friends. Whether they minded or not, hostesses were resigned to the fact that their dances would be invaded, and so tolerated the un-asked guests. A contemporary joke that was thought very funny at the time was the exchange between a mother and her daughter:

'Must I send an invitation to that awful Blank girl?'

'You may as well, Mother. She'll be sure to come whether you do or not!'(32)

As the gate-crasher only chose the best parties to go to, it did work both ways for the hostess, as *Punch* observed:

Ambitious Hostess, (nouveau riche) to her husband: 'My dear, we've arrived! There were no fewer than fourteen gate-crashers here tonight.'(33)

The dilemma of whether or not the gate-crasher should be accepted came to a head at a ball given by the Countess of Ellesmere at Bridgewater House in 1928. Of the three hundred guests that night, a few had been brought along by the invited, as was the prevailing custom. During the dance, Lady Ellesmere rounded on four of the guests whom she did not recognise and asked them to leave, which they did. She then went further and demanded that the 'fullest publicity' be given to the four as a supposed deterrent to the Society gate-crasher in the future. Those concerned, also those not concerned, then voiced their opinions loudly to the Press in what was to become known as 'The Mayfair War'. Lady Ellesmere's ball was undoubtedly a revival of a past era and, as such, should have been treated with due respect. It was a measure of how informal entertaining had become that the majority sided with the gate-crashers. It was said that the hostess did not know her guests personally, so her ball was no different from any other dance during the Season and therefore 'fair game' for the uninvited guest. It is, however, extremely unlikely that Lady Ellesmere did not know her guests. She was forty-eight, the daughter of the Earl of Durham, and very much of the old pre-war order where the hostess made it her business to know every one of her guests.

Where Lady Ellesmere made her mistake was to demand a written apology from the four gate-crashers, one of whom was Cecil Beaton's sister, and another was the new wife of a man who had been invited. A correspondent in the *Daily Express* thought that it was Lady Ellesmere who should apologise, it being 'discourteous, in fact offensively rude, to invite a married man without his wife where other ladies are bidden. As the hostess was unaware that he was married, she was accidently instead of purposely impolite and should surely express regret for this apparent discourtesy.'(34) The leader in the *Daily Express* also sided with the gate-crashers:

> The Ball at Bridgewater House promises to be as famous as the one before Waterloo and to lead to nearly as much fighting. It has often puzzled us why people should willingly go to such affairs, but now the mystery is clear. Where else can they get such fun as at a house where the hostess and half her friends are strangers to one another, where uninvited friends of a fully credentialled guest may be peremptorily asked to leave; where married men who are mistakenly on the bachelors' list may be called upon to apologise for bringing an unasked wife: and where the evening's gaieties are prolonged far into the following day amid a tumult of back-chat, charges and counter-charges, and furious femininities? Formal balls had long seemed to us absolutely zero in the way of indoor sports. Clearly it was our mistake.(35)

Punch's contribution was a cartoon of a man in evening dress, who had been thrown out of some party, marking the portico of the house as a warning to other uninvited guests.

Such was the speed of change that, by the end of the decade, the formal ball (as opposed to the débutante dance) was all but a memory. Many lamented its passing – as an entertainment, Lord Kinross found 'it was aesthetically perfect. Its exclusiveness, its elegance, its dignity made it beautiful. It represented splendour, where its modern equivalent [the late 1920s] represents display. It stood for an idea which was worthy of admiration. It was romantic, noble, exciting to the imagination.'(36) In those few years, it had become a mere shadow of its former self, the haunt of the uninvited guest.

5

THE SPORTING SEASON

'Whose Yacht is it Over There?'

*T*HE LONDON SEASON FOLLOWED a similar pattern to before the war. However, those in Society did not see it as anything special; it was just a period in the year when they went to London for balls and parties, some to Court, like the season when they shot or hunted. To them, it was just a way of life. They automatically went to the Derby, the Royal Meeting at Ascot, possibly Goodwood as well. Between those race meetings were other sporting events which, in varying degrees, were all part of the London Season. High goal polo was almost exclusively played in London. The Eton–Harrow cricket match, known just as 'Lord's' where the match was held, was played in July; the All England Tennis Championships were held at their club at Wimbledon in June, followed, for a few, by the Henley Royal Regatta. The Cowes Regatta at the end of July and the beginning of August officially marked the end of the Season and heralded the start of the grouse shooting season.

During those summer months, between May and early August, there were other events that coincided with the Season, such as the preview of the Summer Exhibition at the Royal Academy in Piccadilly, the Chelsea Flower Show, Covent Garden and the theatre, but they were not part of the Season.

They were, of course, attended by those in Society who were interested in art, gardening, opera or the theatre, but in the main, there were so many parties, dinners and balls that there was not time for any such artistic diversion. Those who 'went to the Summer Exhibition did say, like today, how awful it all was.'(1) At least it provided a topic for discussion at the interminable débutante lunches:

> One could be either artistic (. . . these dreadful moderns . . .) or social (. . . My dear, who *do* you think I met . . .) or sentimental (. . . I wonder if you noticed that sunset in the second room? Quite a little one but I somehow loved it better than anything else there . . .) or portentous (. . . but is that portrait of Mr Baldwin quite *him* . . .?) or merely boastful (. . . well, I suppose it is like the Duke in a way, but knowing him so awfully well, as I do . . .)(2)

Virtually since its inception, no single event has depopulated London more than the Derby, held at Epsom every year since 1780, in the first week in June. It is a traditional Londoners' day out, from members of the Royal Family and London Society down to the thousands of East Enders and gipsies. Unlike Royal Ascot, the Derby has always been more important as a race meeting than a social occasion.

The first post-war Derby brought record crowds, on both sides of Tattersall's rails. They flocked to the Epsom Downs with a brightness that reflected the temporary post-war inflationary boom. In the Members' Enclosure, it was the old pre-war order that prevailed, little different in atmosphere to the last Derby to be run at Epsom in 1914 (the wartime Derby's were run at Newmarket). It was a colourful scene after four drab years. The private boxes were full; a few, as now, turned up in their 'four-in-hands', driven from London by their owners. As one former Epsom steward wrote:

> Memories of the the Derby's of the 1920s come flooding back – all to literally. The weather was atrocious. More years than not, there was a downpour on the day and the mud was almost as bad as in the trenches. We all got stuck. Few of us had set foot on a racecourse for the whole of the Great War, so it was particularly exciting to see such good horses so soon after it. The Army had virtually emptied every stable in the country. Still, I remember a horse broke the course record in '20 [Major Loder's Spion Kop won in the record time of 2 minutes 38.4 seconds]. Everyone was keen to get back to producing some good horses, and they did, too, spending a lot of money.

But the man who really stands out at that time was Steve Donoghue. He had won two Derby's before the war and went on to win three more times . . . He was a wonderful jockey. He was popular too, the crowds loved him. The year he won on Captain Cuttle [1922], a Black Maria drove up the course and a rumour went round that it was that MP who was gaoled for fraud [Horatio Bottomley] arriving for a day's racing!(3)

For the most part, the weather was indeed atrocious. For three years running, 1924–26, it rained solidly all through Derby week. Some drivers went as far as to bring bales of straw on the running boards to save the ignominy, and the expense, of having to be towed out of the quagmire by a willing farmer with a tractor. The traffic was invariably at a standstill, both on the way out and back. 'There were always terrific crowds and you had to leave London before eleven o'clock to get to Epsom on time. The Derby was the most exciting race of the year.'

Where the Derby was an adjunct of the London Season, the Royal Meeting at Ascot was considered by many as its zenith, much to the chagrin of the racing fraternity. Admittance to the Royal Enclosure came through application to His Majesty's Ascot Representative within the Lord Chamberlain's Office, and the qualifications were the same as for Court presentations and levees. As with Court presentations, a far wider circle was eligible for the Enclosure than before the war, which to the 'old guard' inevitably meant a lowering of standards.

As with the first Derby, the old pre-war order was reconstructed for the 1919 Royal Meeting. Not long after the Armistice, *The Times* reported that 'Ascot house agents are already receiving enquiries as to what houses will be available for race week . . .'(4) Such was the competition for houses early in the decade, that prices rocketed. One Ascot hotelier recalled:

The larger houses were let for the week at the most astronomical prices, and the tradesmen – butchers, fishmongers and bakers – just charged what they liked. No items, just a large figure, might be £200 or £300 until someone disputed a bill, and there was a County Court Case and the practice was afterwards dropped.(5)

Throughout the decade, the Royal Meetings were marked, often marred, by the traffic jams in every direction around the course. Would-be race goers would leave London at eleven o'clock on Gold Cup day [Thursday] in the morning and arrive at three o'clock in the afternoon, having walked the last three miles. Apart from the Ascot landaus that brought the Royal party from Windsor Castle, carriages had largely disappeared, but there were a few exceptions such as the Earl of Lonsdale, the 'yellow earl', who arrived in his yellow carriage drawn by perfectly matched chestnut horses, his servants in his distinctive yellow livery. Traffic was directed from an airship, the R36, circling overhead. A racing correspondent from *The Times* was also on board and dropped his copy by parachute every time they passed the airport at Croydon.

Those in the Royal Enclosure aimed to arrive around twelve o'clock in time for lunch. Some had their own boxes where their own imported staff served lunch – not least, of course, the Royal party:

> The Royal Stand luncheon was served by footmen in their leather breeches, and after the first race was over the guests went arm in arm to the luncheon room where small tables, each laid for eight people, clustered round the King's table. At the end of the meal we went, arm in arm, to the ante room and scrambled for coffee . . .'(6)

Those without boxes or houses near the course went to one of the various luncheon marquees they were entitled to. Picnics in the car park also caught on owing to the crush in the luncheon tents. In the immediate post-war years, the tents were mostly from the various arms of the Services. The Royal Navy had their marquee, as had most senior regiments – the Guards, the Cavalry, the Highland Brigade (an amalgam of all the Scottish Highland Regiments), the Royal Artillery, even the Royal Army Service Corps – each with its own mess staff and silver, with NCOs in full dress order at the entrance.

The London clubs also had their own marquees, where women, of course, could be entertained – one year, the Bachelors' Club entertained two hundred débutantes to lunch on Ladies Day. Whites, Boodles, Brooks's and the Turf all had their marquees, as did the other lesser clubs, like the Badminton, Automobile and Conservative Clubs, each with their own servants in their club's livery.

The quality of the racing at Ascot has always been consistently the best, at any time, anywhere in the world. But the Royal Meeting has also been a Mecca of women's fashions. Even before the war, women wore the most outrageous creations, 'clothes we would not have been seen dead in at home. Unlike the Derby and the Oaks, the society magazines and the popular press were full of what Lady So-and-So wore rather than what horse won what race.'

That first Ascot, the 'dresses [gave] a general impression of lightness and flimsiness, predominantly black and white, shading away into cream, dove-colour and grey, lit occasionally by grand splashes of blue, or by pink and yellow.'[7] The writer could have been describing the fashions of today when she noted:

a wonderful sunshade decked with pink ostrich feathers . . . an almost equally remarkable hat with ostrich feathers of brightest yellow, a cloak of Lincoln green which Maid Marian might have worn . . . a black and white chessboard lady, a pink and white spotted lady, a brown and white spotted lady . . .[8]

Nor were the men to be outdone, there were 'Abyssinians in lovely turbans, Serbian officers – their imposing hats that look like a Bishop's mitre cut down – there were also plenty of red tabs which were really pretty things, and can be admired without bitterness by the demobilised.'[9] That year, such fashions were soon spoilt. There was a downpour on Gold Cup day, and the mud was so bad that the women put the straw coverings from champagne bottles over their shoes as they raced to the stands. Like the Derby, the Royal Meetings were dogged by bad weather; a man was even struck dead by lightning in 1930 while sheltering under a bookmaker's umbrella.

So Ascot was marked by the fashions as much as by the racing – in 1924 it was 'very squash-hatty' and, as *The Times* pointed out, it 'is notoriously the best place in England to see beautiful women in beautiful clothes – and also less beautiful women in very odd clothes. I do not hold vaccination marks to be beautiful.'[10] For 1925, the *Times* leader was quick to point out that 'social changes have blurred the distinction between social classes, formerly indicated by dress. Now that money has become a more common standard of value, the old diversity is being replaced by a sameness . . .[11] By the end of the decade, the skirts that had crept higher and higher came down to grass-length Ascot dresses of diaphanous printed chiffon, voile, organdie, or muslin . . . Any woman who appeared in the Royal Enclosure wearing a short dress, which in the previous year was the only correct thing, would have looked completely out of the picture and out-of-date. As *Punch* commented,

ASCOT, AND SO ON
None of the dresses in the Royal Enclosure
(If anybody cares two pins)
Yielded the least trace of exposure
To anyone's shins

The final race meeting that was classed as part of the London Season was the July meeting at Goodwood, a course on the estates of the Duke of Richmond and Gordon in West Sussex, still owned by the present Duke. It is a spectacularly beautiful course, in the lee of the Trundle Hill against the tall beeches of Charlton Woods. As a race meeting, it has always been very different in character from Ascot and Epsom. Being a country meeting and that much further from London, it is naturally less surburban. Edward VII likened it to 'a garden party with racing thrown in' and little had changed since then.

Houses for miles around gave large house-parties for the races, the smartest, of course, being at Goodwood itself. There it was often a Royal house-party, for the Goodwood Meeting was a favourite haunt of George V, as it had been of his father, on his way to Cowes.

One such annual house party that was typical of the time was that given by Lord Leconfield at Petworth House, eleven miles from the course. It was invariably a large house-party. All members of the family turned up as a matter of course, not waiting to be asked. The other guests were invited for their knowledge of, or connections with, racing. The form was the same every day of the meeting; after breakfast, the servants would go ahead to the Leconfields' box and set up the lunch. The house party arrived around midday and repaired to the box. Liveried footmen served pre-prandial drinks on the balcony overlooking the course, followed by a cold lunch in the dining-room. After lunch, the racing members of the house-party went on to the course, while the others cast a desultory eye over the proceedings from the terrace, or visited friends and neighbours in other boxes in the stand. After the racing, they hurried back to Petworth and played 'furious sets of tennis'.

Polo was also very much part of the London Season. The game recovered surprisingly quickly after the war. 'Five hundred players have died on service and in India – the cradle of polo where our best players get their early training – and play has been suspended for over four years, so we have a lot of leeway to make up. Yet despite the number of ponies taken for Army remounts, there are still several first-class animals available, and in a few weeks 180 will be stabled at Hurlingham as compared to 130 in 1914.'[12] By 1920, the three London clubs of Hurlingham, Roehampton and Ranelagh were back in operation. Despite the losses of horses and men, there was still a hard core of very good and keen players – Lord Wodehouse, Colonel H. Tomkinson, Major Locket, General Vaughan, W. S. Buckmaster (founder of Buck's Club) and the Earl of Rocksavage. These and other players were joined each season by the many officers on home leave from India, where polo was a religion. There were also rich polo patrons, like Major Peters, who had two private grounds at his house, Sunbury Manor. Many of the best London teams were made up of '"hired assassins" controlled and financed by some sporting Maecenas – himself generally as keen a player as any of them – who is willing to pay that polo may go on',(13) such as the aforementioned Indian Army officers. One such officer recalled his experience of playing at Roehampton:

> I was not very well mounted and the pony I was riding at the time took fright and carted me off the ground on to the golf course which was next door. Quite out of control, I galloped over the greens to the intense fury and indignation of a number of elderly Colonels who were putting at the time. I eventually regained control and returned to the polo ground to the applause of the spectators.(14)

There were even women players, some more fashionable than skilful, who included Lady Warrender, the Hon. Mrs Norton (later Lady Grantley) and Miss Lexie Wilson.

The International matches between England and America were played over four days in June 1921 at Hurlingham. The American team of C. C. Rumsey, Tommy Hitchcock, J. Watson Webb and J. D. Milburn arrived with sixty ponies. The English team, led by Lord Wodehouse with Colonel Tomkinson and Majors Barrett and Lockett were equally well mounted on thoroughbred horses and a few from the Argentine. The crowd of over ten thousand, that included the King and Queen, the Prince of Wales and King Alphonso of Spain, another keen player, saw England out-played and lose the series of matches.

London polo was not only the best but also fashionable. Vast crowds gathered to watch the matches and the many tournaments. Hurlingham put in new stands to seat three thousand spectators at 3/- a day (£3 for an International Match), but the polo correspondent of the *Country Life*, Scrutineer, dismissed them with:

> The vast majority of those who throng to Hurlingham, Roehampton and Ranelagh have no conception of the difference in the *Entourage* of these fashionable resorts and of polo as played in the Counties. Instead of the mundane crowd, whose attention and conversation lingers more on the fashionable topic or gossip of the moment than in giving anything but the most languid attention to the game. . . .(15)

London polo was over by the end of July, when the top players rusticated to the provincial grounds of Cirencester, Rugby, Dunster, in Somerset, or Cowdray, in Sussex, particularly during Goodwood Week, which coincided with their important tournament.

The Eton–Harrow match was held annually in Long Leave (mid-July). It had always been an intensely social occasion since its inception in 1804. It was the best attended match of the season at Lord's, with tens of thousands of spectators and dozens of carriages lining the boundary. It was, and is, quintessentially English, and totally unintelligible to foreigners. One Frenchman, invited to Lord's, charmed his host when he timidly asked, when another Eton wicket fell, what the game was all about. When he was told, he inquired, '*Alors, c'est Harrods qui gagne!*'(16)

'As a society fixture it ranks high, and as a purely cricket event it has long been regarded as one which may well furnish the Gentlemen, and even England, with future players'.(17) The standard was high, and many an illustrious man today rates playing at Lord's as the highest achievement of his life.

For centuries, the rivalry between the two schools has been intense, both at School and after. Lord Home remembered the exchange between the Prime Minister, Stanley Baldwin (Harrow) and his Home Secretary, Bridgeman (Eton). The Prime Minister made some disparaging remark about Eton which 'Bridgeman did not judge to be up to standard. He bided his time. One morning at Cabinet the Prime Minister congratulated the Home Secretary on the rapid ending to a serious riot in one of HM's prisons. "How did you do it, Home Secretary?" he asked. "Oh, Prime Minister, it was very easy. I just told the Governor to order the prison band to play 'Forty Years On' [the Harrow School song], and the prisoners stood to attention and quietly returned to their cells.'"(18) Often, the rivalry at Lord's erupted into a little 'top-hat bashing' at best, a full-scale riot at worst – the fight at the 1922 match is still quoted by peers in the House of Lords during debates on soccer violence.

The enthusiasm for Wimbledon in the 1920s was every bit as keen as today, particularly among women spectators. Centre Court seats were at a premium, especially before the club moved to its present, larger site. Those who were not members had to ballot for seats. Members were at a premium too: in Hans Duffy's novel, *In England Now*, a particularly odious man is being discussed and the protagonist replies:

'Yes, I suppose it's time I began looking him up again, his great charm being four perfectly good centre-court seats every day at Wimbledon.'
'How can you bear him for five seconds?' said Rose.

'He only occupies one of the seats, and kind friends take it in turns to be buffers. Besides which, you must admit that you always come yourself when I invite you.'(19)

Those who flocked to the Centre Court found the game dominated, as it is today, by foreigners – Americans, like 'Big Bill' Tilden and 'Little Bill' Johnson, the French players like Henri Cochet, Jean René Lacoste and the woman who initially captured the public imagination, Suzanne Lenglen. She reigned supreme for seven years, from 1919 to 1926. She was a genius on court, some say artistic. She was also accused of lack of sportsmanship, so vital in that amateur world, on account of 'her unorthodox behaviour, her tantrums and her hysterics'.(20) Her clothes were as important as her play. She dispensed with petticoats and long sleeves, advocating 'a simple *piqué* dress, or one of drill or white linen, made in the old Grecian style, or fastened at the waist with a ribbon or leather belt. The sleeves should be short. A simple pair of canvas "gym" shoes are best.'(21)

Although it has always been assumed that Henley Royal Regatta was an essential part of the London Season, as indeed crowds flock there today, in the 1920s it was very much an acquired taste, peopled only by the rowing *aficionados* or those on the fringe of Society. At its height, towards the end of the Victorian era, Henley had been a popular event, with dozens of house-boats and launches moored along the course. After the war, the house-boats had gone and the Regatta was in serious financial trouble. The new Enclosure was made into a club, available to anyone who was proposed and seconded. The die-hard old rowing men complained bitterly in the Press that they were being squeezed out, 'and the Regatta given over to the social butterflies'.(22)

Where it was comparatively simple to try to recreate the pre-war order in most social and sporting functions, no one seriously believed that the 'Big Class' yachts could possibly be revived after the war, on either side of the Atlantic. But the lead was taken from the King. He was persuaded to bring his beloved cutter, *Britannia*, then twenty-eight years old, out of retirement and re-rig her. It was a difficult decision. Such expense could easily be seen as extravagance, but the King believed it would stimulate others and so give employment to countless craftsmen. His lead was followed by Sir Thomas Lipton who brought out *Shamrock*, Sir Thomas Allom with his *White Heather*, Mrs Workman with *Nyria* and the financier Clarence Hawtry with his American schooner, *Westward*. Mr R. Lee actually commissioned a new cutter, *Terpsichore*, 'at a cost of twenty-four thousand pounds [now £360,000] especially to race against the King'.(23) With the return of the 'Big Class', others followed. Old steam yachts found new owners; cruising and racing yachts were restored and new ones built. Within two years of the end of the war, the sport was revived. Other great yachts were built throughout the 1920s, such as the 93- ton cutter *Moonbeam*. The most important of all venues was Cowes, on the Isle of Wight, especially during 'Cowes Week' that fell during the last week of July and the first week in August immediately after Goodwood. At Cowes, the only place that really counted was the Royal Yacht Squadron.

It was often said, particularly during the premiership of Lloyd George, that it was easier to enter the House of Lords than to become a member of the Royal Yacht Squadron. It was one of the last strongholds of the old order, although none of them was the owner of a first-class racing cutter. Those belonged to tradesmen. 'Tommy Lipton, the grocer, Sir Charles Allom, the antique dealer, Sir Howard Frank, the estate agent, Lord Waring, the shopkeeper, W. L. Stevenson, the chain-store chairman, Sir William Berry, the newspaper proprietor, Hugh Paul, the maltster, Tom Sopwith, the aeroplane maker, T. B. Davis, the ex-stevedore, Mortimer Singer, the sewing-machine manufacturer – all names from the world of finance, but none of them, when they first be-came owners of large yachts, members of the RYS.'(24) For some inexplicable reason, the committee and members found brewers and distillers acceptable. The King himself had to put the strongest pressure on the committee when he heard that the Lord Chancellor, Lord Birkenhead, was about to be blackballed.

'Cowes Week' was a perfect venue for 'those on the way up', who were able to race against the King in person and to fraternise with other members of Society. Like today, there were balls and parties, the smartest, of course, being 'The Squadron'. The King entertained on the Royal Yacht, *The Victoria and Albert*, or one of the two guard ships.

Besides the Royal Yacht and the Royal Navy guard ships, there were many large motor and steam yachts, including one owned by the Duke of Westminster. His yacht, the *Cutty Sark*, was built as a destroyer and half finished when the war ended. She was then converted by the Duke, later to be immortalised by Noël Coward in *Private Lives* in the exchange:

'Whose yacht is it over there?'

'The Duke of Westminster's, I expect. It always is.'(25)

After 1926, the final race of the week was around the Fastnet Rock, off Ireland. By the time even the fastest yachts had returned from the race, the migration to Scotland and the north of England for the grouse shooting had begun.

The spread of the railways to Scotland in the mid-nineteenth century brought the rich Victorian sportsmen to the Highlands. When Queen Victoria bought Balmoral for Prince Albert, the migration north, to some, acquired a fashionable image – the aristocracy, however, were rarely influenced by the Royal Family. Either way, London was deserted by Society from early August onwards, a rustication that lasted until the Great War. Once again, it was feared that the war would have finished the annual Scottish invasion from the south. The moors suffered from neglect, but after 'a couple of seasons, they were back in condition with plenty of grouse.' The deer forests hardly suffered at all, and after the weaker stags were culled, the stalking was as good as ever.

The Scottish land-owners with their vast Highland estates came out of virtual 'hibernation' at the start of the grouse shooting season, popularly known in the Press as the 'Glorious Twelfth'. English land-owners who also owned estates in Scotland travelled north and were joined over the next twelve weeks by assorted family and guests. The majority of hosts were those who took or rented a lodge, a Scottish term for what could be anything from a very large, furnished house with a grouse moor, a deer forest and a salmon river, down to a rather 'primitive house without electric light and a farm track to the front door'.

To the delight of the Scottish owners, their lodges were much sought after by the richer Americans. They paid fortunes for their sport – as much as £7,000 [now over £100,000] was the going rate for a three-month let; one American put down £35,000 for a five-year tenancy of a famous moor. Scotland rang with stories of American extravagance – one brought 450 pairs of sheets in order to save on the laundry. Such lavishness was short-lived – after the Wall Street Crash these extravagant rents dried up.

At the end of the Scottish Season, the families and their guests drifted back south; some returned to London for what became known as the 'little Season', while the land-owners returned to their estates for the winter.

6

LIFE IN A COUNTRY HOUSE

'That Wretched Tallulah's Got my Flower'

*W*HATEVER THE DELIGHTS, real or supposed, of the London Season, a period which even in its heyday lasted only three months, the English are by nature a race of country dwellers. The history of England, unlike France, does not lie in her capital, but in the countryside. While the French aristocracy fawned at the court of Versailles, the English aristocracy were, and are, truly at home on their estates, mindful of their feudal obligations to the land and the people. In England, land-owning has always been the basis of the aristocracy, whatever the source of the wealth created to buy that land – politics, trade or, later, industry, as with the profiteers of the Industrial Revolution. The new rich established themselves and their families by buying estates, and 'by the second generation their families had absorbed from the soil the character, the manners, and the qualities of the aristocrat'.(1) Once they had assumed the full responsibility of all that owning an estate entailed, then, and only then, were they accepted into the ranks of their neighbours.

To an Englishman, land-ownership is a way of life – 'Land Owner' was a perfectly acceptable entry as an occupation or profession on a British passport. The love of the land is bred into an Englishman, it is something that he never loses. Lord

Beauchamp, ruined by his vindictive brother-in-law, the Duke of Westminster, who had instituted the warrant for his arrest on homosexual charges, did manage to return to England for the funeral of his son, Hughie. In the few hours he spent at Madresfield Court, Lord Beauchamp was seen in the very early morning wandering round his estate and garden, renewing, for what he believed to be the last time, his ties with the land his family had owned for centuries.

The Edwardian era was the zenith of country house life. Even then, the stability and permanence of the system – where 80% of the land was owned by 3% of the people – was being eroded. The knell began as early as 1909 with the Finance Act that increased taxation on all land-related revenues, which in turn precipitated a gentle move to sell off agricultural land, even whole estates. By 1913, a Parliamentary committee was set up to examine the causes, and it found that:

> in the opinion of the majority of witnessess who appeared before the Committee, the increase in the number of agricultural estates which have recently been offered for sale is partly due to a feeling of apprehension among land-owners as to the probable tendency of legislation and taxation in regard to land. Whether this feeling of apprehension is well founded or not, it undoubtedly does exist.(2)

Landlords began to fear what future legislation could do to them, although at that time there was no evidence that they had been adversely affected. One answer was to increase the rents (that were generally below their economic value), but the easier option was to sell. With a sale, any mortgage could be paid off and the landlord was free of his financial burden and moral responsibilities.

In the years immediately after the First World War, it was estimated that eight million acres in Britain changed hands, far more than at any other time in history. One firm of estate agents claimed to have sold within a year an area the size of an English county. *The Times* carried an article in 1922 entitled 'England changing hands' which mentioned a firm of estate agents with 79,000 acres on their books: '7,650 acres of Lord Manton's land in Suffolk and 31,000 acres of the Duke of Hamilton's property were up for sale'.(3) Estates were sold off in Scotland as well – when one northern land-owner bought part of the Duke of Sutherland's estate in Caithness, he climbed to the top of the highest mountain with the factor and pointed to what he wanted. Back in the estate office, the boundaries on the map were drawn up, the acreage worked out and charged at 2/6d (12½p) an acre.

Such sales were caused by a number of factors, not least the same pre-war fear of penal taxation – there is a family story that the 8th Duke of Rutland went white at the mere mention of the word. Income tax, that accounted for barely 4% of the rent-roll before the war, increased to over 25% by 1919.

The Central Land-Owners Association made representation to the Chancellor of the Exchequer over the effect taxation was having on agricultural estates and on their owners:

> Individual land-owners in large numbers have, much against their inclination, been forced to sell their homes as their only alternative to insolvency, and it has been estimated that 700,000 acres of agricultural land have been disposed of annually for some time past . . . [such] sales only mean transfer of ownership. Many of the new owner-occupiers have been forced to borrow for the purpose of purchase, and their first experience of ownership under such heavy burdens is to find themselves without the necessary funds to work their land properly or to make any expenditure upon capital improvements . . .
>
> . . . the land-owning class, which has done great service to the country and has never failed it in an emergency. The class is now in imminent danger of complete destruction, and it is respectfully submitted that the burden of taxation upon agricultural land is unfair and confiscatory, and calls for immediate redress.[4]

The plea was received sympathetically, but it did not affect the final issue.

That much of the land was bought by the tenant farmers was hailed as 'an historical romance, prophesying that henceforward the people of England would own England'.[5] Many of these farmers were undercapitalised and were to founder a few years later in the agricultural depressions. Others, of course, survived, especially the war profiteers and other new land-owners with money to ride out the depression. In 1921 an article entitled 'Changing hands; a Note of Resignation' appeared in *The Times*, in which a correspondent hoped that in the change of ownership the spirit of the place and the traditions of the country house could still be preserved. The new incumbents were given some salutory advice:

> The newcomers must not be disappointed; at first it will be hard for them to realise how much personal work is needed to make a large, or even a moderately sized country house run smoothly. The mere engagement of a first-rate house-

keeper and butler entrusted with the selection of the under-servants, and a free hand as to wages, will not fulfil their new responsibilities. If they are eager, partly from a sense of patronage, partly from a desire to help others, to make efforts towards personal benevolence, they must not be surprised if at first they meet with a cold reception. With the demesne they have not purchased the humbler dwellers on it. Only let them beware of committing the un-pardonable crime of not appreciating the wonderful treasure they have acquired. Let them really live in the old house for the greater part of the year, fit up the nurseries . . . There lies the clue to England's well-being in the future. Let the new generation blend the new ideals and aspirations with the old experience and traditions – then, though England will have changed hands, the old spirit will remain.(6)

The war brought great sacrifice and hardship to all levels of society, but none more lasting than to the landed families with their traditions of military service. Many land-owners had been killed in the war, leaving the problems of paying off death-duties and of running the estate to the widow or young heir. Often it was the heir himself who was killed:

In the useless slaughter of the Guards on the Somme, or the Rifle Brigade in Hooge Wood, half the families of England, heirs of large estates and wealth, perished without a cry. These boys, who had been brought up with a prospect before them of every good material thing that life can give, died without complaint, often through the bungling of Generals, in a foreign land. And the British aristocracy perished . . .(7)

With the direct heir killed in the war, disheartened parents often saw little point in carrying on with an encumbered estate, and opted out by selling.

Occasionally, the reason for the sale of an estate was merely the high price of land at that time, with many land-owners just 'cashing in' their estates to live on a more certain income without responsibility. Some kept just the house and park, others sold them off separately for schools or other institutions. A great many houses were pulled down – a continuance of the destruction of the country house which had been started in the late nineteenth century.

Whatever the financial situation of the land-owners, they invariably complained that they were ruined – in most cases, however, they were just marginally less rich. The Marquess of Lansdowne's economy to counter rising costs was to do with one less footman – he was, however, immediately re-employed as the Marquess was giving a lavish ball and could not do without him. Colonel Wyndham made do with a parlour maid, as they were twenty pounds a year cheaper than a butler. An economy, used by many families then and since, was to give up *The Tatler, Country Life* or *The Sketch. The Spectator* went so far as to publish a series of articles in 1921 on 'How to save the country houses of England', which, among other suggestions, advocated opening them to the public. They did not go quite so far as Colonel Blount in Evelyn Waugh's *Vile Bodies* who, complaining of the high bus fares, let out his house for filming.

But despite these 'swingeing' economies and land sales, life in the majority of country houses and estates went on very much as before the war. Generally, the older the family, the more likely they were to keep their estates. The editors of *Burke's Peerage* and *Burke's Landed Gentry* found that those whose estates dated back to the twelfth and thirteenth centuries fought harder to keep them and generally succeeded; those who failed were generally the descendants of Victorian industrialists who had bought their estates a generation or two before. However, many of the landed classes were dispossessed and, despite the loss of their estates, they were still included in a separate section of *Burke's Landed Gentry*. Over a thousand families were described as 'late of' or 'formerly of' their property. By 1937, only a third of the families listed actually held land, whereas the figure today is nearer to a half.

Some land-owners could go 'plucking' to survive – pictures 'plucked' off the walls, or other valuable objects, were sold to the ever eager American market. It was reputed that £175,000 was paid for Lady Desborough's 'Madonna and Child', £417,000 for the Holford pictures and £63,336 for the Britwell Library. Lord Sackville was able to stay on at Knole solely through selling his better pictures. London houses went before land – the Duke of Devonshire sold Devonshire House in Piccadilly for £1 million before he parted with a single acre of his Chatsworth Estate. The Marquess of Salisbury sold his house in Arlington Street, which had been in the Cecil family for generations, for £120,000 to Lady Michelham: he was, however, able to buy the house next door for £60,000 when 'the market had eased'.

The shrewder land-owners made their estates into limited liability companies soon after death-duties were first introduced, notably the Duke of Buccleuch, the Earl of Moray and Viscount Novar. Others simply married money, often American money – sometimes twice, like the 8th Duke of Marlborough – in the manner of their Victorian and Edwardian forbears.

While parents could be distant, Nanny was always there, and for many remained an intimate friend for life. The joy of discovery on the seashore.

A gaggle of nannies in Kensington Gardens, probably comparing notes about their employers and their charges.

Mother sometimes joined in too. A sense of stability on the promenade deck of an Orient liner.

An ordeal manfully borne. Gavin Astor, a child of the twenties, leaving a Society wedding with his mother, Lady Violet Astor.

Opposite: *Eton days.*
Above: *a family picnic on the Fourth of June.*

'The Super Fag' – cartoon by H. M. Bateman.

Below: *it's the Fourth of June, and a newish Etonian shows his sisters around town.*

The independent airs of
Eton. **Left**: *the 'Pop Room',
where members of the elite
Eton Society keep in touch
with the world outside.*

Above left: *arriving at Lord's
with parents and more
hampers for the Eton-Harrow
match.*

Above: *a leaving breakfast.
It used to be said that there
was an Old Etonian in every
Embassy and every gaol in
every country. What does the
future hold for the class of
1926.*

Right: *members of the Eton
Society returning for their
last term.*

Sebastian Flyte's epic lunch party in the
Granada Television production of Brideshead
Revisited. Sebastian (centre) was played by
Anthony Andrews. On his left is Anthony
Blanche (played by Nicholas Grace), and on his
right Viscount ('Boy') Mulcaster (Jeremy Sinden)
and Charles Ryder (Jeremy Irons).

Brian Howard, precocious aesthete at Eton and
Oxford, outrageous leader of the Bright Young
People, and prototype for Waugh's Anthony
Blanche. Caricature by 'Angus' in the Cherwell.

Opposite: pogo sticks were all the rage in 1924.
This Cambridge undergraduate has got the right
end of the stick but nevertheless seems to have
missed the point.

The Oxford Union Railway Club, photographed
with porters on one of their expeditions. Middle
row (left to right): Michael Rosse, John Sutro,
Hugh Lygon, Harold Acton, Bryan Guinness,
Patrick Balfour, Mark Ogilvie-Grant, Johnnie
Drury-Lowe. Back row: Henry Yorke, Roy
Harrod, Henry Weymouth, David Plunket-
Greene, Harry Stavordale, Brian Howard. The
club, which was founded by John Sutro, became
a rallying-point for the Aesthetes and lasted
until 1939.

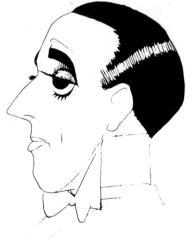

ANGUS

King George V and Queen Mary, with their children. From left to right: the Prince of Wales (later Edward VIII), the Duke of Gloucester, the Duke of York (later George VI), Prince George, later Duke of Kent. Seated on the left is the Princess Royal. By the end of 1918 their Court had regained its pre-war splendour.

Débutantes at Queen Charlotte's Ball at the Dorchester – the excitement apparently no match for the tension.

The lack of servants immediately after the war was not felt so acutely in the country as in London, where the alternatives to domestic service, when available, were more lucrative and less restrictive. Also, when a family stayed in their London house, they generally took their staff from the country. In the country, both indoor and outdoor servants tended to be either very old or of school age – those in the middle had either been killed in the war or opted for a less servile life in town. With the general agricultural depressions throughout the decade, both men and women drifted back into service. No house of any size could do with less than a butler, cook, house maids and chauffeur; if there were children, then a nanny and nursery maid as well. The outdoor staff would include a head groom, possibly two under grooms if the whole family hunted, a head gardener and an under gardener. Grander houses obviously had an army of staff, when they were available, the ultimate being the Royal Household. When George V was recuperating in Bognor he took the minimum of staff. At a private cinema show in the house, he was joined by this skeleton staff – forty-five servants of varying rank. Concurrent with the shortage of servants came the new labour-saving devices which obviated the need for quite such a vast staff. The vacuum-cleaner did the work of an army of house maids; commercial laundries did away with the house laundry and the need for laundry maids; electricity dispensed with the endless chore of cleaning and filling oil lamps. However, apart from the bathrooms, there was no plumbing upstairs, so water still had to be carried to the bedrooms, and the slops carried down in the morning.

To the majority of the land-owning classes, it was the pride in the actual ownership of their estates, rather than the love of the land, that was of paramount importance to them. Nancy Mitford in *The Blessing* described it 'as a most tremendous luxury, owning land. There was never any idea of making it pay.'(8) The estate, house and land together, was a sacred inheritance, to be handed down from father to son. In *A Handful of Dust*, Evelyn Waugh encapsulated that sacrament in the conversation between Tony Last and his wife over her suggestion that it was pointless to live in a house the size of Hetton:

I [Tony Last] don't keep up this house to be a hostel for a lot of bores to come and gossip in. We've always lived here and I hope John will be able to keep it on after me. One has a duty towards one's employees, and towards the place too. It's a definite part of English life . . .(9)

Beyond that, the majority knew, or cared, little about estate management. Apart from providing them with an income, woodlands were for holding pheasants to shoot (unlike the French who 'have foresters in their forests, not just gamekeepers');(10) fences were 'cut and laid' to jump out hunting, and so on.

There were, of course, exceptions. The Marquess of Bath, who, as Lord Weymouth, inherited the estate (not the house) at Longleat, cared 'passionately' about his land. 'I knew every field and wood, and all the tenants too, farmers and cottagers alike.' Mindful of his inheritance, he attached himself to the land agent on an estate near Wantage to learn something of estate management before he took over in 1928. The 11th Duke of Bedford 'regarded himself as something of an innovator in agriculture and forestry, and wrote one or two books on the subject which I [the 13th Duke of Bedford] believe are classic examples of how not to run such matters'.(11) The 8th Duke of Buccleuch was a renowned silviculturalist who, throughout his life, was frequently mistaken for a forester as he worked in his woods.

Estates of any size were managed by a resident land agent, known as a factor in Scotland, who may have been, but more likely was not, a qualified member of the emergent Land Agents' Society (now part of the Royal Institution of Chartered Surveyors). They were drawn from a variety of backgrounds – impoverished land-owners or those, like Lord Weymouth, about to inherit an estate of their own, often a friend from the regiment from the war, sometimes an upgraded farm bailiff.

The home farm was managed by a farm bailiff, who, 'as you knew nothing about farming, tried to lose you less money than if you managed it yourself'.(12) There were, of course, exceptions, but it was still thought ungentlemanly to be a farmer. With the various depressions in farming throughout the twenties, it was difficult to let a farm, so the land-owner had to take vacant farms in hand to keep them going. The idea was that the home farm would provide fresh meat and dairy produce for the house, for both family and staff, in which it generally succeeded, but at a price. Such were the farming losses that some unscrupulous land-owners went in for 'slut-farming' – those with 'sufficient private means not to worry about making their farms pay. They left their fields to get full of thistles and even thorn bushes, which provided cover for game; and found rough-shooting far more fun than un-economic farming.'(13)

In the 1920s, social life in an English country house largely revolved around the other members of the family and guests asked to stay, topped up by the more genial of the neighbours. Nancy Mitford's Lady Montdore 'filled Hampton every weekend . . . but, so great is the English predeliction for country life, she generally managed to get these visits extended from Friday to Tuesday, so she was left with two empty days in the middle of the week'.(14) The norm, however, was from Saturday to Monday, which was also the contemporary term for a weekend. The house party often centred around some sporting event as well, such as a race meeting, a day's hunting or a shoot in the winter, or a cricket match in the summer.

It is, of course, impossible to generalise on the enjoyment, or horror, of a country house 'Saturday to Monday', no two houses or hosts being the same. With a beautiful, fully staffed country house, a Saturday to Monday could be well ordered, comfortable, active and great fun, an experience not shared by all. A different recollection of the period is that

a married couple arrived in their own car with a chauffeur and ladies' maid. The chauffeur and ladies' maid sat in the back, the married couple sat in the front. The wife generally drove. If it was a shooting weekend, the chauffeur might act as loader for his employer, otherwise his duties were merely to bring the car to the front door, take it back to the garage, service it and clean it. The chauffeur/valet has never existed outside the pages of period novels and homosexuals' reminiscences. The husband would not, unless he was very grand, bring his own valet as his butler would act as valet at home and a butler had to be left at home to see that the resident staff did not nick the silver in their employers' absence. The host's butler and footmen would act as valets for male visitors. This entailed removing the clothes they had discarded when they changed for dinner for brushing and pressing and returning them to their owners' bedroom when they called at nine o'clock. This time-honoured habit has been known to oblige guests of a religious turn of mind to attend early service in their dinner jackets as, at eight o'clock, no other garment was available. No well-trained servant would answer a bedroom bell rung before the hour for knocking on the door and drawing back the curtains. Who knows what they might have discovered by such premature invasion of privacy! Breakfast was partaken from nine-thirty onwards.

The wife's clothes travelled in a trunk which was fixed to a rack at the back of the car and designed to look, when in place, as if it were part of the vehicle. It had to be a large trunk as it was full of tweed suits and twin-sets and lots of flounced evening gowns or dresses with floating panels that creased easily. Every woman travelled with at least eight pairs of shoes. This was necessary as, like the men's day clothes, shoes were whisked away and cleaned by a man especially employed for this purpose. Unfortunately, it did not seem to be his job to return them to their owners, which meant that unless the owners had many reserves they had to come down to breakfast in their gold, kid, evening slippers and go for a wet country walk in their nice leather court shoes. They were lucky to get them back before their cases were packed to leave.

It was necessary for the women to take their own maids as these employees knew exactly what their mistresses intended to wear and when and laid the requisite garments out on the bed. Girls who shared a ladies' maid with their mothers had, when visiting alone, to make do with the services of their hostess's housemaids. These were invariable fiendish women of warped mentality who unpacked for the defenceless female guest and hid her clothes in places she would never think of looking for them, like in the cupboard in the bathroom or the top drawers of some old tallboy standing in a dark corner of the bedroom. Chests of drawers were always full of eiderdowns or blankets or somebody else's clothes mislaid from a previous visit. For dinner, the fiend-housemaid would lay out on the bed either the guest's nightdress or a lace petticoat. These women had to be lavishly tipped for causing a weekend of constant humiliation, anxiety and embarrassment. However, the footmen were generally better looking and more amusing than the average male guest. It was quite permissible for a female guest to crack a joke or two with him while he was helping her on or off with her Newmarket boots.(15)

With or without guests, the daily routine for the family of a country house was virtually unalterable. This was partially due to the servants, whose meal-times were rigid, and partly, in the early years of the decade, as a hang-over from the formality of the Edwardian era. Family and guests were called at nine o'clock with the cup of tea that had been ordered by the hostess the night before. It was brought by the guest's personal maid or the 'fiend' housemaid for the women, the valet or footman for the men, when they came to draw the curtains and raise the blind. In the winter it was a chilly start, as only in the grandest houses were fires lit in the bedrooms.

Daily life was regimented by the four meals, each one large by comparison with today. Breakfast was considered a major meal. The contemporary novel, *In England Now*, opens with a typical English country house breakfast scene:

The dining-room at Skroton Hall is pleasant to enter when the sun pours down in a shower of gold on the breakfast table, mingling with the brightness of the honey and the marmalade, and reflected back in dazzling sparks from the silver and glass. In the shadow, with the sombre complacency of the man who knows he is indispensible and can afford to bide his time, stretches the white length of the sideboard. As the eye travels along that serious array of victuals and drink, and realises the number of covered dishes, each over its little flame, the cold meats tricked out in parsley and jelly, the urn of porridge, the jugs of cream, the steaming pots and kettles, the tins and packets of patent food, thinning, fattening, sustaining, you think of the inadequacy of human powers when faced with infinity. The sideboard is old, as old as the house, and nowadays sags slightly in the middle, bowed by the burdens generations of Sidebothame footmen have laid on it for generations of Sidebothames to devour.(16)

The silver dishes, heated by spirit-lamps burning under a row or copper hotplates, contained all sorts of breakfast fare, such as 'eggs cooked in various ways, bacon, sausages, kidneys, mushrooms, kippers, kedgeree.'(17) There was cold fare on the sideboard as well, 'ham and tongue, and game pie if you wanted it'.(18) It was a fluid meal; unless there was some special reason for an early breakfast, such as shooting or hunting, it began around nine-thirty and went on until eleven-thirty.

Lunch was served in the dining-room at any time after one o'clock – at least after the servants had had their lunch. This was another large meal; an egg dish or similar to start, followed by 'a main course, followed by cold meats on the sideboard if anybody wanted them; pudding; cheeses; and dessert'.(19) Lunch was always an informal meal, with guests and family often helping themselves. Only in the very grand houses were there servants. In the summer, there were often picnics, either on the estate or nearby. These were popular not only with the guests but also with the staff, who were, of course, left behind.

Thus fortified, the family and their guests were set for the day. The good hostesses were skilled enough to organise their guests without them feeling that they were being organised. Naturally what was on offer depended on the season and the house. The most popular summer entertainment was tennis. The standard of tennis was directly proportional to the state of the court. Every country house of note boasted a court, some of them, where there were serious players, more than one. These courts were nearly all grass, hard courts still considered a rather vulgar novelty. The Duke of Westminster had two outside courts and an indoor clay court, housed in an enormous building with a resident professional on hand at all times. Lord Birkenhead, a fanatically keen player, organised tennis tournaments at his house, Charlton, just outside Oxford.

Croquet was another perennial game, played everywhere with enthusiasm. Golf was also popular for both men and women. Some houses, including all the Royal country residences, had their own golf courses. There were also a few houses with squash courts but cricket was the principal game that was played with great enthusiasm all over the country. The keen cricketing families had their own cricket grounds – some, like the Leigh-Pembertons at Torry Hill, in Kent, and the Earl of Carnarvon at Highclere, still play on their own grounds today.

Many house-teams were made up entirely of the family and a few friends and neighbours. Others, like that at Hatfield, had an estate team, drawn from the family (the Cecils), and their indoor and outdoor staffs. Occasionally, the land-owner played for the village team. Whatever the team, the estate usually provided the cricket pitch.

Swimming pools, particularly heated pools, were also a novelty. Sir Philip Sassoon installed a beautiful pool at his new house, Port Lympne; the Duke of Richmond and Gordon had one installed at Goodwood, although 'everyone disapproved of it. They thought it was rather fast'. Lord Beauchamp had a pool at Madresfield, where he

> managed to introduce an air of ceremony even into the bathing parties. 'The ladies' were expected to leave the water first. When they had gone, Lord Beauchamp would turn to the gentlemen and say: 'The ladies have left us, you may now lower your costumes' – by which he meant they could bare their chests and roll their bathing dresses down to their waists.[20]

Wet-weather entertainment was much the same in winter and summer – a long damp walk, or a ride. Crazes came overnight, and disappeared just as fast. Pogo-sticks made a brief appearance in 1924; roller-skating in 1926. The basement passages at Lord Astor's Hever Castle were thought ideal for roller-skating, and many a guest spent a bruised Saturday to Monday as a result. Lord Glenconner enjoyed it so much that he built a rink of his own at Glen, his neo-baronial seat in Peeblesshire.

Tea was another serious meal. It was served either in the drawing-room or, more usually, in the dining-room. 'It was an awful bore to have tea in the drawing-room as you had to stop what you were doing while the servants set up the folding table, laid it and brought in all those rattling plates.'(21) It had to be a very grand house for the women to change for tea, the practice having died out in most houses before the war.

In the more traditional houses, men and women spent their day (outside meal-times) apart, so games of billiards, occasionally snooker, were played in the afternoon, or between tea and dinner. To play after dinner (as in bad period films) would have been rude to the hostess and insulting to the other women.

Everybody, of course, changed for dinner. A gong sounded just half an hour before a second one, which announced dinner. The family and guests went up, hopefully for the bath that was drawn for them, and to change into the clothes that had been laid out in front of the fire lit some time earlier. 'It never entered your head to do anything for yourself – some people even had their clothes put on for them.'(22)

For dinner, women's fashions changed throughout the decade. Dresses that started and finished the decade long, rose to the knee in between. Pyjamas for dinner were a thirties invention and only worn for dinner with family and close friends. The men wore dinner jackets, the host sometimes wearing a smoking jacket. In the very grand houses, everyone was expected to wear a tail coat. At Petworth, Lord Leconfield always dined 'in white tie and tails. When a gentleman came to stay with only a dinner jacket, and apologised for not having brought his tail coat, Uncle Charles [Lord Leconfield] would offer what he thought sage advice: "You should sack your man." It never entered his head that some of his guests might not have valets.'(23) The 9th Duke of Rutland also insisted on white tie at Belvoir, even for a small family dinner. Michael Tennant, the Duke's brother-in-law, asked him if they never wore black tie in the country, to which the Duke replied, 'Yes, when I dine alone with the Duchess [Michael Tennant's sister] in her bedroom.'(24) Lord Beauchamp went even further and entertained regularly at Madresfield Court. When there was a house party he would come down to dinner wearing the blue ribbon of the Order of the Garter across his chest.

Before dinner, family and guests gathered in the drawing-room where they were given a drink. The sherry of the early twenties was soon replaced by cocktails, generally served by the host from a tray brought into the drawing-room. Some families considered a drinks tray in the drawing-room vulgar and so left it on a table outside. The standard and quantity of drink obviously varied from house to house. While Sledmere, in Yorkshire, was famous for the strength of the Sidecars (brandy, cointreau and lemon juice) mixed by Sir Richard Sykes's butler, Cassidy, there were other places, such as Longleat, which were practically dry. Cocktails were unheard of at Longleat, so Henry [Weymouth, now the Marquess of Bath] made them secretly in his rooms at the top of the house, where we all met at six o'clock. We had arranged a plan in case of an interruption, and this was successfully put into operation when Lord Bath made an unexpected appearance. Henry had a bastard sealyham which was a wicked fighter: its arch enemy was Charlie Brocklehurst's shaggy mongrel. As Lord Bath opened the door Henry kicked the two dogs together, and, in the hullabaloo that ensued, whisked away the cocktail paraphernalia while we all hid our glasses.'(25)

In the country, no one was escorted into dinner but there was, of course, a *placement*, with neighbours slotted in between the house party and family. During dinner, a footman, or whoever else's job it was, removed the drinks tray and glasses, tidied the drawing-room and made up the fires. It 'never entered your head how much easier it would have been to throw a log on the fire and draw the curtains yourself. Instead, you just rang the bell and the footman did it for you. It always took an age for him to come.'(26) Being called, the footman never knocked.

If it was a grand dinner party, as opposed to just a family dinner, a typical menu began with 'either thick or clear soup, followed by fish, followed by an entrée – chicken or quails. Then you had saddle of lamb or beef; you had pudding; you had a savoury; and then you had fruit.'(27) There was sherry with the soup, white wine with the fish, red with the main course. For a more informal family dinner, the entrée might be left out. Coffee was served in the dining-room, and when the hostess had finished her cup, it was time for the women to leave. The men stayed on smoking and drinking port for at least an hour. The party was then united in the drawing-room for some form of post-dinner entertainment. Games, like bézique, backgammon and bridge, and others more frivolous, took the place of conversation: the less highbrow the house, the more physical the games.

By the early twenties, contract bridge had become so popular that it was practically a mania. A form of bridge had been brought to England by Lord Brougham from Cairo as early as 1894; auction bridge came from India in 1903, for which the Portman and Bath Clubs standardised a set of rules. Contract bridge, a derivative of the French game, *plafond*, replaced auction bridge as the social game soon after the war, when the cards committee of the Portman Club fixed the rules. Women played in the afternoon, both in London and the country. Men were just as dedicated:

> You sat by electric light at the same table, hour after hour, going through the same motions, thump thump thump . . . life passed by, the things of the mind neglected, the beautiful weather out of doors unfelt, unseen. 'One club, two no trumps. Three spades. Four spades. Game and rubber. I make that one rubber of sixteen – pass me the washing book, old boy.'(28)

Although card games for money were disapproved of in Royal circles, even the King had to bow to popular taste and allow a 'few tables in another room' after dinner at all the Royal residences, but guests were not joined by members of the Royal Family. Most games were played for small stakes, to steady the game, but there were those who played for seriously large stakes, traditionally at clubs like Whites, the Portman and the Bath.

Mah-jong was equally popular in the 1920s. As a game, it considerably predated bridge. Originating from China (*ma-tsiang* means sparrows, an analogy to the clicking of the little bamboo and ivory domino-like pieces and bone 'money'), it arrived 'in time for the Christmas market' in 1923. The West End stores were full of expensive sets; several books were published on how to play. It was *the* Society game, and for the short time the craze lasted, drawing-rooms the length of the country resounded with cries of Chinoiserie terms – 'Pung', 'Kong' and 'Chow' when particular sets were completed, or talk of North or East Winds, Red or Green Dragons. Newspapers carried mah-jong columns giving advice on play: 'Don't forget to say "mah-jong" [to end the game having won] very quietly and with a restrained air. The moral effect is doubled' . . . 'Don't either lie or speak the truth consistently'.(29) Reporting the first mah-jong tournament in Kensington, *Punch* took a more jaundiced view of the game: 'It is still hoped that the outbreak may be localised'.(30) Everybody played; Beverley Nichols recalled the dialogue of Lady Diana Cooper playing mah-jong with 'Oggie' Lynn, Tallulah Bankhead and their hostess, Gracie Ansell:

> *Oggie*: 'Oh dear! That wretched Tallulah's got my flower.'
> *Tallulah*: 'Well dahling, you've got my wind.'
> *Gracie*: 'Diana's made a gong [*sic*] of the prevailing wind and *I* haven't got any winds or dragons or anything.'
> *Lady Diana*: 'It isn't the prevailing wind, darling. East's prevailing.'
> *Tallulah*: 'No dahling. West. (Suddenly) *Pong!*'(31)

Other after-dinner entertainment varied from house to house. Large and difficult jig-saw puzzles intermittently occupied many hours over the weekend for the whole house party. Anne, Countess of Rosse, always had one on the go, 'because then you were bringing people together. A lot of romances started over those jig-saws.'(32) Crossword puzzles appeared for the first time in 1924 under the name of 'crossword squares' – *The Times* only starting theirs in February 1930. One critic of the twenties called the crossword 'the symbol of the age: an inexpensive and ostensibly harmless amusement, leading – nowhere. Utopia in seven letters.'(33)

'Paper' games, both intellectual and frivolous, were another source of amusement, at least to the family. Each house had its own games, at which the family, naturally, excelled, but which for shy guests meant agonies of embarrassment. As at Oxford, there were Aesthete and athlete houses. At a typical 'Aesthete' weekend in 1929, Cecil Beaton was one of the guests at Stephen Tennant's house, Winscote in Wiltshire. After dinner they played 'Analogies' and 'Interesting Questions'. Beaton recalled being 'very bad at that [the latter], being so ill-educated. But, by dint of being funny instead of knowledgeable, I managed to come out fairly well. Stephen Runcimen wrote about me: "My mother: Lady Colefax. My father: Cardinal Mazarin. My teacher: Leonardo da Vinci. My governess: a piece of porcelain. My skeleton in the cupboard: a kind heart. What would I save from the fire: myself."'(34) The idea, of course, was to guess from the answers who the person was.

Other houses went in for acting games like charades, where the whole team performed together, and 'the game', where each person went singly. Some families went further, like the Bromley-Davenports, at Capesthorne in Cheshire, who put on their own plays in a private theatre in the house.

Practical jokes were also much in vogue – apple-pie beds and creatures in the bath were thought highly amusing. More enjoyable than anything, though possibly not for the hosts, were the endless children's games of Sardines and Murder.

Amongst the younger members of the family and their friends who lived in London during the week, a Saturday to Monday was merely an extension of their London life, and that meant dancing. In the less formal country houses, the carpets were rolled back, the gramophone wound up, and they danced all afternoon and evening, breaking only for meals. The very grand houses with huge house parties, like those of the Duke of Westminster at Eaton Hall, imported a local band for their guests to dance to after dinner.

When family and guests wearily returned to their rooms, the fire had been made up, their beds turned down and their day-clothes removed. What is a constant memory of the period is 'watching the shadow of the flames on your ceiling before falling asleep. Unless, of course, it was somebody else's ceiling which was much more fun.'(35) As with every age, 'corridor-creeping was tremendously exciting, particularly if you were put at one end of the house and the girl was at the other. You had to be jolly careful in the morning too: not to get caught in her room any more than to be missed in yours.'(36)

7

THE PURSUIT OF EXCITEMENT

Huntin', Shootin', Fishin' and Flyin'

*A*PART FROM THE AFFAIRS OF HIS estate, a small part of a land-owner's time was taken up with the traditional works that were expected of him, the likes of Justice of the Peace, possibly Lord Lieutenant or Deputy Lieutenant of the County, High Sheriff, honorary Colonel of the Yeomanry, Chairman of the local Conservative Party or, like Lord Brideshead in the absence of his father, president of the country agricultural show. The rest of his time was taken up with amusing himself and his guests, occasionally his children. Once the chalelaine had given instructions to the cook and house-keeper, dealt with the head gardener and arranged the flowers, her public life in the village or county was as much or as little as she cared to do. The rest of her time was for her own enjoyment. In the winter months, the sportier families and their guests hunted, shot or raced, or combined all three.

Nearly half a million horses had been taken from the English countryside to the Great War. Apart from the few favourite chargers brought back by officers atbarrass their own expense, the horses remained in Europe. Half of those taken were hunters, but despite this mass depopulation of every hunting stable in the country, packs of hounds did survive. The (9th)

Duke of Beaufort, chairman of the Master of Foxhounds Association, maintained that 'The great thing is not to let any hunt cease to exist.'[1] Small nuclei of hounds were kept for breeding after the war, or to hunt, when and where possible, to control the fox population. Horses were scarce, fodder and food were in short supply, and the hunt servants were either very old or very young. In an unprecedented move, women also became masters of packs of foxhounds, either in place of their husbands on active service, or in their own right.

After the war, hunting was revived as quickly as the kennels and stables could be restocked, and it was not long before it was at something approaching its pre-war standard. Serious hunting was affected neither by the agricultural nor the economic depressions of the decade. At Melton Mowbray, in Leicestershire, the metacentre of the 'Melton packs' (the Quorn, the Cottesmore and the Belvoir), it was the hunt and its subscribers, with their huge demand for fodder and supplies, that kept the farmers and tradespeople going through the more difficult times.

Lady Marchmain in *Brideshead* would have been miserable at Melton Mowbray, for she

> always detested hunting because it seemed to produce a particularly gross kind of caddishness in the nicest people. I don't know what it is, but the moment they dress up and get on a horse they become like a lot of Prussians. And so boastful after it. The evenings I've sat at dinner appalled at seeing the men and women I know, transformed into half awake, self-opinionated, mono-maniac louts![2]

Throughout that period in the 'Shires' (predominantly Leicestershire), everyone, practically without exception, hunted. They existed solely for the sport, their lives revolving entirely round their horses. The field was mixed. There were those who remembered, and lamented, the passing of the golden age of hunting before the war. There were 'any number of them, people like the Phillips of Old Dalby Hall, Darby Wright of Saxby and Phillip Cantrell-Hubbersty at Ragdale who had owned, and still owned, estates in the [hunting] country'.[3] There were others who took houses in the country for the season, both serious 'hunting folk' and a large proportion of pure social climbers who regarded hunting as an entry into Society. Evelyn Waugh, who hunted enthusiastically for two years, admitted later that he disliked it, adding that he did it 'only for social reasons'.[4] 'New money' could fraternise quite happily with the landed society out hunting, though they would never be asked back to dine, at least for a generation. There were even two hunting parsons; one was known as 'the Dasher', and the other, the Reverend Seabrook from Waltham-on-the-Wolds, 'went' particularly well.

Although Leicestershire had offered the finest hunting in the country, it was the Prince of Wales who made the Shire packs smart to a certain element known as 'carpet-baggers'. He began hunting with the Pytchley, in neighbouring Northamptonshire, immediately after the war and soon gravitated to the faster and racier Melton packs. In 1923, he took a suite of rooms at Craven Lodge, an uninspiring, red-brick, hunting guest-house in the middle of Melton Mowbray. It was owned by Mike Wardell and run by his step-father, Major-General John Vaughan. Melton's standing was raised even further when he was joined by his youngest brothers, Prince Henry and Prince George – the Duke of York preferred the less social Pytchley. The Prince of Wales kept his rooms until 1929, when the Queen and the Prime Minister, Ramsay Macdonald, both urged him to give up race-riding after a series of crashing falls. After that, hunting lost its appeal to him.

Well before the season began in early November, horses were brought in from summer grazing. Special trains were hired to bring 'outsiders' horses to Melton Mowbray. Strappers or grooms, one to two or three horses, were hired at 38 shillings a week (the equivalent of £30 today), which included lodging but not food. The houses for miles around filled up. Hunting boxes, often grand country houses, were taken on long leases, some only occupied for the season. Sir Victor and Lady Warrender, for example, took Lord Gainsborough's Exton Park; Ambrose Clarke, enjoying an almost limitless fortune from Singer sewing machines, took Warwick Lodge, where he stabled his fifty thoroughbred hunters; while Lord and Lady Furness took Burrough Court, the house where the Prince of Wales first met Mrs Wallis Simpson. Every house in Melton Mowbray was also full: 'doctors, dentists, anyone with a half-decent house, let it for the season'. The owners moved out and the 'carpet-baggers' moved in with their servants. Craven Lodge was always full, booked from one season to the next. There was not a spare box in Melton Mowbray or for miles around the town; every livery stable and yard was filled with literally thousands of hunters. The Army also had, and still has, its Remount Depot at Melton Mowbray, much to the delight of the Cavalry officers who flocked there during the Season.

Estates were bought in the country, again solely for the hunting, both before and after the war. For example, the Marquess of Blandford bought Lowesby from his brother, Lord Ivor Churchill, while the Londonderrys had a place at Oakham.

The twenties were a halcyon time for those 'Meltonians'. In theory, it was possible to have six top-class days a week from

Melton Mowbray: the Quorn on Mondays, the Cottesmore on Tuesdays, the Belvoir on Wednesdays, the Quorn again on Fridays, and the Belvoir and Cottesmore alternatively on Saturdays – other days with those hunts were bydays which were less crowded and also in less good country. Thursday was generally a byday, but those keen enough could go to the Fernie in South Leicestershire. Some did manage the six days, but four or five was more the norm.

There was a seemingly inexhaustible amount of money about. Everyone spent freely. The subscription in the middle twenties for three days a week with any of the packs was £100 (the equivalent of £1,500 today, double the subscription for one day a week with the Quorn). In the early twenties, subscribers gave just what they could afford. But the subscription was negligible compared to the other costs of their hunting. They were all generally well mounted, many having yards of between thirty and fifty horses for their families. There were plenty of horse-copers to choose from – 'Drage, the Young brothers, Beebe and Sam Haymes from Somerby'.(5) Some had their own 'masters of the horse' – Ambrose Clarke employed Reg Hobbs to see him well mounted – while others relied on the eye of their stud groom. The real hunting people bought their own horses, often from those who were hard up and financing their hunting by selling on young horses they had made during the season. Dress was immensely important: the hunting people and 'carpet-baggers' alike turning up immaculate at a meet, save for the Prince of Wales who wore his hat at a ridiculously jaunty angle.

On a good day with any of the Melton packs, it was not uncommon to have a field of four hundred followers – a smart, but lesser, pack like the Fernie, would not have half that number. During the season, the meet was generally at eleven o'clock. Many would have hacked anything up to twelve miles from their houses to the meet, but the majority would have sent their horses on with a groom and arrive by car. If it was a lawn meet, they would be offered a glass of sherry or port before moving off to draw the first cover. Each pack had a professional huntsman. A master who hunted hounds himself, like Major Tommy Bouch of the Belvoir, was an exception and not generally approved of either. Like the subscribers, the masters fell into two camps – those with the money and those 'of the country'. The most popular of the latter was the Master of the Quorn, Major 'Algie' Burnaby, whose family had lived at Baggrave Hall. His former claim to fame was to win the first Moonlight Steeplechase. He was a hard gambling man, who was saved from his final ruin by a rich American wife. The 'moneyed' masters were men like Gordon Colman of the Belvoir (whose family made their money from 'what the aristocracy left on the side of their plates', i.e. mustard); Sir Harold Nutting, who joined Burnaby with the Quorn, and whose family bottled Guinness; and Major 'Tommy' Bouch, Master of the Belvoir, whose family fortune came from constructional engineering.

Once hounds had found and were running, the field opened up:

In those days, the hunting was pure magic. Those who rode well, were well mounted and knew the form, were immediately off at the front. For many, hunting was a pure science. They were tremendously knowledgeable and enjoyed it enormously. They loved to see hounds work. They would watch for all those tell-tale signs, cattle moving on the top of a hill, and so on. The Prince of Wales was not one of them; he was uncertain in his seat but he had any amount of guts. [Major Burnaby would check any man riding too close to hounds with 'Come back, young feller. Who the hell do you think you are – the Prince of Wales?'(6)] On the best days it was all grass, nothing but good, galloping grass, not a ploughed field anywhere. In the ten seasons of the twenties, I should think I rode across perhaps three ploughed fields [on the best days only]. They were all stock farms, fat cattle and the odd sheep, all on small fields properly fenced with timber or nicely cut-and-laid hedges. You could easily jump eighty fences in a day, not a strand of wire in the place. Some fences had the added excitement of a deep ditch on the landing side that you couldn't see, while some had a deep ditch on both sides.

The foxes went well too. The earth stoppers always did a good job, so off we went. There were few cars on the roads, unlike today, or foot followers either, so the fox was rarely headed. You kept very quiet and out of the way if you followed in a car and only went on foot if you'd broken something.

By about one o'clock, some of the field had had enough and gone home. Lionel Tennyson would be on his way to London by then! You found your second horse, if you were lucky enough to have one, by about two o'clock. Often, if the fox ran out of that day's country, you would be miles from the second horses and have that dreadful 'hound jog' back to where you thought they would be – most second horsemen just followed the hunt second horses as they knew in advance which coverts were being drawn.

With a field of four hundred, there were anything up to a hundred and fifty second horses clattering around the roads. The second horsemen of some of the grander families, like the Londonderrys, the Lowthers or the rich Harrisons, were dressed in livery; the rest in smart, grey whipcoard suits. Strapped on to their saddle was your lunch in a sandwich box and a flask if you thought you were going to find them; if not, you took it with you to the meet.

Hunting finished at dusk. The more fortunate found their way to the village post office and rang home for a car. The chauffeur brought one of the grooms who rode the horse home. The alternative was to hack home, often miles and miles. Sometimes, if your horse was tired, you had to walk it back. We did not mind, it was all part of the fun of hunting.[7]

Horses were everything. Even when there was a frost and there was no hunting, General Vaughan opened up his indoor school at Craven Lodge and barked at people while they went over a few jumps.

'The "Meltonians" were very competitive: they competed for the best horses, the best men and the best women.'[8] They hunted hard and played hard. The Melton Mowbray of the twenties was the epitome of that carefree age. While the old-school hunting families kept their own company, eschewing the more raffish members of Society and certainly all new money, the Melton set had few such inhibitions. Affairs were rife during the hunting season, and a constant source of gossip. There were parties every night — vast dinner parties, impromptu dances, small dinners. The conversation was always the same — horses and hunting. They gambled heavily, mostly poker and bridge.

There was a party every Saturday night at Craven Lodge. They were wild, abandoned affairs, always with plenty to drink. 'There was dancing on the piano, a lot of noise. We all had the greatest fun.'[9] There were cabarets, either put on by the guests, or well known performers like Douglas Byng were brought in. Often there was a theme to the party: a baby party, a circus party, a clown party, a drag party, or, as described in the local newspaper, a nursery party:

The ballroom was converted into a nursery, with nursery pictures and rhymes decorating the wall, and all the guests dressed as small children, and carried favourite toys. The hostess welcomed her guests dressed in a frilly frock of pale organdie muslin and hugging a Teddy bear. Captain Player wore a sailor suit. Captain Sam Ashton was little Lord Fauntleroy in a velvet suit with bare knees; Major Jack

Harrison was an Eton boy; Lord Northland was a schoolgirl in a short red check frock and black curls; and Lady Brownlow, Lady Anne Bridgeman, the Hon. Edward Greenall, and Miss Monica Sheriffe were schoolgirls in party frocks, socks and corkscrew curls.[10]

When the hunting season finished at the end of March, the horses were put out to grass and grooms and strappers were dismissed, leaving just the stud groom and possibly the better second horseman. The yards in Melton Mowbray emptied; special trains took away the horses to all parts of the country for the summer. Craven Lodge was silent. There were no more parties. 'The summer in Melton was like Bond Street in August.'[11]

Of the hunting and the life in 'High Leicestershire', Miss Monica Sheriffe recalled wistfully, 'We had it too good. I still can't believe it after all these years.'

No other hunt really compared to the Melton packs, although some came close to it. When cheap Canadian and American wheat flooded the cereal market and so depressed the English price of corn, farmers went into livestock, putting their land down to grass, which, in turn, made for better hunting.

There were a few private packs of hounds, the best known being the Beaufort. The 10th Duke of Beaufort inherited his father's hounds in 1924. He kept a fully-staffed stable of fifty horses, even employing his own full-time blacksmith, and hunted from the middle of August to 1 May, six days a week. The 3rd Lord Leconfield kept his private pack until after the Second World War. When one nervous young man asked him at breakfast, 'What hounds are you going out with today, Lord Leconfield?', he merely replied, 'My own.'[12] There were also private packs of stag hounds, such as Lord Rothschild's at Waddesdon, who hunted 'carted deer'. Lord Redesdale, immortalised as Uncle Matthew in *The Pursuit of Love*, hunted his children with a pack of bloodhounds. The story is slightly apocryphal, however, as there was only one bloodhound.

With the difficulties of transporting horses before the war, guests asked to hunt were either mounted by their hosts or provided with hirelings. After the war, only in the grandest of houses were the guests mounted. Shooting was a different matter, and, unless a neighbour, everyone invited to shoot was invariably asked to stay in the house. However, 'houses wherein a party of eight or ten guests, plus wives and daughters and ladies' maids, valet, chauffeur and loader are accomodated without inconvenience or comment are no longer so numerous . . . [13]

Like hunting, the great shoots had suffered during the war. The majority of the able-bodied keepers were naturally called up, so there was little keepering or rearing of pheasants for four years.

After the war, the shoots were built up again and restored to something like their pre-war glory. Shoots were generally held mid-week, the beaters being drawn from the estate staff. In the grander houses, including the Royal country residences, the keepers were dressed in smart green uniforms with brass buttons, breeches, gaiters and a bowler hat, trimmed with gold braid and acorns. The beaters were decked out in white smocks. There were many first-rate shots (George V was one of the top six), who travelled round the country during the season, shooting anything up to six days a week. The bags in the twenties were considerably less than those of the *grandes battues* of the Edwardian era, there being many fewer pheasants put down. The standard and the quality of the shooting, however, were vastly superior.

Women generally joined the guns for lunch, sometimes held in the dining-room, but more often in an outlying tenant farmer's house, where the food was brought up by the footmen. A shooting lunch was generally a simple meal, like a stew and some plum pudding. The better shoots served beer and cider, with port or cherry brandy after. The women then joined the guns at their stands after lunch. They had to be 'very keen, or very much in love, to go out any earlier'.(14)

Those who fished in the twenties (and thirties) experienced exceptional fishing. 'There was any amount of first class [salmon] fishing to be had all over the country, but especially in Scotland. There was extensive fishing in Ireland too.'(15) Of the Scottish rivers, the east coast were held to be the best, from the Naver down to the Tweed. Riparian owners invited their friends to stay and to fish their rivers; those without rivers, or friends, could easily take a beat on practically any river of their choice. Agencies, like 'Captain Percy Wallace's Sporting Agency', had dozens of fishing lodges in Scotland for rent, and fishing hotels, with access to good rivers, were plentiful and inexpensive.

Most were spring rivers and fished from the end of February until the end of June – the autumn run coinciding neatly with the 'Scottish Season'. Everything about the fishing was marvellous:

The fish were bigger, and there were more of them. Most rivers were well keepered and only the odd salmon 'for the pot' was poached – then, there were few cars for the poachers to carry their heavy nets around, and there was no lucrative outside market for a poached salmon. Salmon were safer in the sea too – there was no netting and the seal population was a mere 2,000 as opposed to 84,000 today.

As the fishing was so plentiful and inexpensive, it was more relaxed. You didn't fish nearly so hard. You would wander out at about ten in the morning, most likely with a gillie to each rod. If you were in by five, that was it. If the weather or the river were not in fair-fishing-order, then you didn't bother to fish. You changed for dinner and didn't go out again. Not like today when you've paid a fortune and have to get your money's worth. It was thought very *infra dig* to sell your salmon at the end of the day.[16]

The equipment of the twenties fisherman was also good, although the Hardy split cane salmon rods tended to be longer, as much as eighteen feet, and thus heavy. They were also inexpensive – £1 per foot, less for a greenheart rod. The line was oil-dressed plaited silk with a silk trace; the flies were nearly all feather, the serious fishermen tying their own.

Like the great shots, there were men who did nothing but fish, going from river to river, either as owner, guest or tenant. George McCorquodale of Tuchan Lodge, took nearly 9,000 salmon out of the Spey alone. Robert Pashley, known as the 'Wizard of the Wye', lived at Walford, near Ross. In his fishing life, he killed nearly 63 tons of salmon. In one year, 1926, he killed 535 salmon in a season: once killing eighteen salmon in a day.

Generally, fishing and house-parties did not go together, but there were a few exceptions, like Gordon Castle, on the Spey, where the fishing was taken seriously. 'Before a day on the Spey, the fishing lunches were a great business. At breakfast, the side tables groaned with food. French rolls were piled high, waiting to be filled every kind of cold meat and game. Nothing was more fun or more amusing, in the opinion of the guests, than the performance of selecting and cutting your own fare for the day.

Grouse, ham, beef, and every other joint of bird or beast in season were dismembered, or sliced, to be cut up or minced – needless to say, very badly by amateur enthusiasts – whilsts rolls were split and filled to bursting point . . . Jammy buns were a feature of these feasts.'[17]

The two technical developments that made the greatest difference to life in the twenties were the wireless and the motor car. While the car to most families was merely a form of transport, the sportier models were for fun or racing. There was a great choice. Apart from the many car-manufacturers of the day, there were 'dozens of small coach builders who put a sporty looking body on a basic chassis, and then tinkered with the engine to make it go faster. Some were even supercharged.'(18) Many of the famous makes of the sportier cars, like Bentley and Morgan, have survived today, but the majority have gone.

Although cars and motor racing did not have the same cachet as field sports and racing, or the same Society following, they did at least have an enthusiastic following. Hill climbs (where the contestants raced against the clock rather than against each other) were immensely popular. 'In those days you could go to the local police chief and get them to close a road for the day. There used to be a regular fixture between Oxford and Cambridge. They were great fun. It all stopped when some lunatic in a Bugatti got out of control and killed some spectators.'(19)

Motor-race meetings were popular, attracting vast crowds from all walks of life. Some, as observed by Evelyn Waugh in *Vile Bodies*, were 'knowledgeable young men with bright jumpers tucked inside their belted trousers, old public school ties, check tweeds, loose mouths and scarcely discernible Cockney accents'.

With only two motor-racing tracks in England – Brooklands, in Surrey, and Donington Park, in Leicestershire – the sport was dominated by the Continental drivers and car manufacturers: 'speed kings of all nationalities, unimposing men mostly with small moustaches and apprehensive eyes'.(20) Motor-racing was taken more seriously on the Continent, hence their superior cars and professional drivers, while in England it was still an amateur affair, a 'close-knit group of friends with a mechanical bent'. The Hon. Frederick Guest, a competent driver himself, was an early president of the British Racing Drivers' Club. He was succeeded by Earl Howe who was 'a great man, a ferocious driver, very powerful on the track. He had his share of accidents too.'(21) Like the Hon. Brian Lewis (later Lord Essendon), he drove foreign cars, while the Earl of March (the present Duke of Richmond and Gordon) was loyal to the British makes, mostly MGs and Austins. After winning one 500 mile race at an average speed of 83.5 mph, he became a 'works' driver for Austin.

Although private flying was still in its infancy, it was surprisingly popular in the twenties. Surplus planes were sold off after the war; many more were built at the well-known aircraft factories, like Sopwiths and de Havilland. Some were even designed and built by amateurs. Flying schools sprang up all over the country, which were later consolidated into the National Flying School Company with the Hon. Frederick Guest, himself an owner/pilot, on the board of directors. He also employed a professional pilot, 'Mouse' Fielding, who was later seconded to the Prince of Wales when he bought his own Gipsy Moth. The Prince's plane was modified 'to take his several suitcases, a hat box, golf clubs and walking sticks.'(22) Fielding also taught Prince Henry and Prince George to fly.

The Duke of Richmond and Gordon, who learned to fly in 1929, found flying in the twenties 'great fun and very relaxed. You saw a nice pub and a handy field beside it, so down you went.' In the mid-twenties, scooters were all the rage. Sir Philip Sassoon, 'due to some confusion of the accelerator with the "stop" lever, spelt death to his [riding] habit . . . and he shortly afterwards purchased and learned to fly an aeroplane'.(23) Sir Philip was extremely rich and a totally fearless flyer. He used his plane principally to fly between his two estates, Port Lympne in Kent and Trent Park in Hertfordshire, 'flying most of the time at ground level, hopping over hedges'.

Women became avid flyers too. Miss Rachel Wrey, later Lady Willoughby de Broke, piloted her own plane from Sywell in Leicestershire. Lady Bailey obtained her pilot's certificate in 1926, and within two years was not only the first woman to fly solo across the Irish Sea but also had the world altitude record of 18,000 feet. Later, she flew to Cape Town and back, navigating from a small-scale map on the back of a travel agent's brochure. The Duchess of Bedford, who became known as 'The Flying Duchess', found that the change in atmospheric pressure while airborne alleviated the buzzing in her ears. She began flying in 1926, later buying her own plane and employing a commercial pilot, Charles Barnard, part-time to fly it. They went on longer and longer flights, until, in 1927,

> the Duchess, with her pilot, in a Moth aeroplane flew from her place, Woburn Abbey, to Paris, Biarritz, Madrid, Seville, Tangiers, Toulouse, Lyons, Paris and London. She crossed three ranges of mountains, the Pyrenees, the Guadaramas, and the Sierra Nevada.

> 'I went for the scenery alone,' the Duchess of Bedford continued, 'and that has been wonderful beyond description. As you see, the little Moth has returned without a scratch – and the same may be said of its passenger. There is none of the dust, dirt and fatigue of ordinary travel and I return as fresh as when I started . . .'

> The Duchess of Bedford, who is in her sixty-second year, is an enthusiastic air traveller. She enjoys not only straight flying but also aerobatics. Before landing at Stag Lane yesterday, her pilot put the machine into a spin and executed some steep Imelmann turns.(24)

Soon, she took out a pilot's licence herself and bought a larger plane, employing Barnard full-time. In 1930, they flew to Cape Town and back, the trip taking just seventeen days. It was an adventurous journey that, among other excitements, brought them down in the jungle in the Sudan. On their return, they received a great welcome. At the age of seventy-one, the Duchess needed just fifty minutes to complete two hundred hours of flying time. She set off on a solo flight in her Gipsy Moth, but was caught in a snow-storm, crashed in the sea, and was never seen again.

But flying was not the prerogative of the rich. The most famous flyer of the day was Amy Johnson, a working-class girl, who broke the solo record with her monumental flight to Australia.

8.

THE SOCIETY HOSTESSES

'Hands up the
Next Ranking Dook!'

*A*MONG THE MOST MARKED OF the many differences between pre-war Society and that of the 1920s were the background and fortunes of those women who ruled their particular sections of that Society, especially. London Society, and its very *raison d'être*. Up to the end of the nineteenth century, the principal function of Society was political. Politicians, like Ralph Nevill, recognised its immense importance, writing that 'the social functions of the London season are almost as important as meetings of the Cabinet'.[1] Disraeli appreciated the consequence of politics and Society; in one year alone, he entertained 450 different people to dinner. Traditionally, the Whig and Tory hostesses kept rival establishments. Newcomers to Parliament depended on political dinners as the only place where they could meet their chiefs. By the mid-1880s, the Souls, a group based on pure intellect rather than party, had been formed and, for the first time, political opponents met on a social basis. But the great hostesses still flourished – the Primrose League was born out of Lady Dorothy Nevill's Sunday luncheons; the 'Double Duchess' (the Duchess of Manchester later married the 8th Duke of Devonshire) held considerable political power.

Edwardian society was primarily engaged with its 'fast life', of affairs, shooting parties, racing and baccarat, and took little interest in politics. Mrs Sackville-West thought that they believed that

> politics were children that they trusted to the care of nurses and tutors, remembering their existence from time to time, principally in order to complain of the inefficient way the nurses and tutors carried out their duties; but although they were careful to give an impression of being behind the scenes, like parents who go up to the nursery once a day, their acquaintance remained oddly remote and no more convincing than an admirably skilful bluff. It was founded on personal contact with politicians; 'Henry told me last week . . .' or 'A.J.B. [Arthur Balfour] was dining with me and said . . .' but their chief desire was to cap one another's information.[2]

The role of the political hostess had virtually died out after the war. Lady Astor surrounded herself with politicians, but many stayed away out of dread of lemonade. Lady Wimborne kept a quasi-political salon, but, although the General Strike was settled at her luncheon table, she did not pursue her political aims. The most notable exception, was the Marchioness of Londonderry, wife of the seventh Marquess.

On the death of her formidable mother-in-law in 1919, Lady Londonderry took over as Society's most influential hostess. Once again, Londonderry House and the 'Londonderry House set' continued as the centre of the social side of the London political scene, a scene dominated by the new Marchioness. Her nickname of 'Circe' was suggestive in its implication, and her admirers over whom she cast her 'spell' were many and diverse. Her greatest conquest was undoubtedly the Socialist Prime Minister, Ramsay MacDonald, so much so that a Labour MP was heard in a lobby of the House of the Commons to mutter, 'A few months ago he sang the Red Flag. Now he whistles the Londonderry Air.'[3]

On the eve of each Parliamentary session, Lady Londonderry gave a huge reception, often with as many as fifteen hundred guests. It was every social climber's dream to mount the broad, sweeping staircase to be received by the Marchioness, tall and stately, invariably wearing the famous Londonderry tiara, rubies and long, drop earrings. Her inner sanctum of friends were members of what was called 'The Ark', or the 'Marchioness's bestiary', the members having their own special names. Her husband was 'Charley the Cheetah'; Lord Hugh Cecil was

'Charley the Lynx'; Carson was 'Edward the Eagle'; while Churchill was 'Winston the Warlock', and so on. Invitations to parties were engraved:

YE ARCHAIC ARK ASSOCIATION
Londonderry House, Park Lane.
Her Arkship, Circe the Sorceress,
commands the attendance of
....
at a feast to be held in the Antediluvian
Dining-den of the Ark.

Today, such a 'club' appears trivial, but at the time, it wielded great influence and many hoped, in vain, for an invitation to join. Besides these political gatherings, Lady Londonderry gave many other balls, dinners, intimate supper parties and receptions – the young Captain Harold Macmillan (the present Earl of Stockton) and Lady Dorothy Cavendish held their wedding reception at Londonderry House. The great virtuosi of the day, men such as Chaliapin, Rubinstein, Rachmaninoff and Kreisler, all performed at her weekly musical evenings.

'The greatest political hostess of her day' gave her last reception at Londonderry House shortly before her death in 1958. The guest of honour was the then Prime Minister, Mr Harold Macmillan.

Before the war, political and non-political Society was led by the old and aristocratic families, families like the aforementioned Londonderrys, the Greys and the Cecils. Apart from a few notable exceptions, the successors of the famous Victorian and Edwardian hostesses such as the Ladies Shaftesbury, Waldegrave, Spencer, Pembroke, Stanhope and Derby, and all the duchesses, were pale imitations of their mothers- and grandmothers-in-law. In the twenties, the Duchesses of Portland, Beaufort, Rutland, Devonshire, Buccleuch, Somerset and Richmond all entertained in their London houses, but not in the grand manner of pre-war days. Only the Duchess of Sutherland gave an annual ball, but it was generally in keeping with the vogue for fancy-dress balls of the times. The Duchess of Bedford cared only for flying; the Duchess of Marlborough's only interest was dog breeding. With the 'Social field' virtually clear of the aristocratic hostesses of the old order, the gate was open for a new breed of women to take their place. This was achieved by either sheer weight of money (coupled with great presence, for money was never thought to be enough on its own), or by possessing the majority of those qualities described by John

Lehmann, who knew all the hostesses in the twenties, and who declared in his autobiography:

A great hostess and creator of a salon needs an unflagging curiosity about other people, a flair for making them feel at home, or at least stimulated in her circle, almost unlimited time to organise her entertainments and to devote herself to the pursuit and domestication of those rising celebrities her shrewdly selective eye has marked down; and plenty of money.(4)

There were a few families (mostly new money), who entertained as lavishly in the twenties as they had in the late Victorian and Edwardian eras, families such as the Rothschilds, the Sassoons, the Monds and the Ludlows, but the past-mistress of them all was the Hon. Mrs Ronald Greville.

Like Sir Walter Raleigh in *1066 and All That*, Mrs Ronald Greville 'was left over from the previous reign',(5) but, unlike Raleigh, she was as much a force in Society after the war as before. When she made the classic remark to Beverley Nichols, 'One uses up *so* many red carpets in a season!',(6) she was quite genuinely referring to entertaining her real friends, who were members of most of the royal houses in Europe, not least the Royal Family. Queen Mary gave Mrs Greville her friendship; the Prince of Wales stayed at her country house, Polesden Lacy, in 1922; but her biggest coup was to lend the house to the Duke and Duchess of York for part of their honeymoon.

For the illigitimate daughter of a self-made Scottish brewer, James McEwan, this close friendship with Royalty, not to mention the widest possible selection of the aristocracy, politicians and diplomats, was social climbing par excellence. Although she had an inexhaustible supply of money, a titled husband at Court (the Hon. Ronald Greville was a friend of Edward VII), she carved herself out a considerable position in Society through her character and forceful personality alone. 'One could hate her, fawn upon her, be amused by her, but one could not ignore her or feign indifference to her'.(7) Cecil Beaton described her as 'a galumping, greedy, snobbish old toad who watered at her chops at the sight of Royalty and the Prince of Wales's set, and did nothing for anybody except the rich.' Some of Beaton's observations were undeniably true, but not all. She was spiteful and malicious, she had an acid tongue, yet she was extremely generous, always anonymously, to deserving charities.

Mrs Greville, or Maggie as she was known to her friends, was left one and a half million pounds by her father. Her suspect origins did not embarrass her – she once declared that she would rather be a beeress than a peeress. Besides keeping a close watch on the source of her wealth, the brewery, she dedicated her life and considerable fortune to entertaining. Her two houses, one in Charles Street, Mayfair, and Polesden Lacy in Surrey, were virtual shrines to entertaining and the last word in opulence and comfort. All the guest bedrooms at Polesden Lacy had bathrooms 'en suite' – a rare luxury at that time. Her dinners were lavish, particularly if Royalty were present, even if the service was poor. Her butlers, Boles and Bacon, were often drunk. At one dinner for the Yorks, Osbert Sitwell recalled that the evening was 'like jazz night at the Palladium. All the butlers were drunk – since Maggie was ill – bobbing up every minute during dinner to offer the Duchess of York whisky.'(8) To her lasting embarrassment, at another dinner even she noticed that her butler was drunker than usual and pencilled him a note reading 'You are drunk. Leave the room at once'. Boles then placed the note on a silver tray and staggered round to the guest of honour, Austen Chamberlain, who looked at it in horror and remained silent for the rest of dinner.

Right up to the Second World War, Mrs Greville continued to entertain in the grand manner. At Charles Street there were anything from ten to sixty people for dinner, and, of those, often fifty were titled. The Duke of York, later George VI, was frequently the guest of honour. Weekends at Polesden Lacy were more modest affairs with around fourteen people to stay, house-parties that, besides the Royal Family, often included foreign Royalty, for example the Queen of Spain, and the Kings of Greece and Egypt.

Harold Nicolson, who had thought of her as 'nothing more than a fat slug filled with venom', once asked, 'How comes it that this plump but virulent little bitch should hold such social power?' Such a position was understandable before the war, when the Edwardians thrived on those outward displays of opulence, on gossip, and on *salons* filled exclusively with the aristocracy, Royalty, statesmen and men of power, regardless of intellect. In the twenties, the Society in which Nicolson moved had more to offer, was more sensitive and was a great deal more amusing. Mrs Greville proudly told her friends that 'You mustn't think that I dislike little Lady Cunard, I'm always telling Queen Mary that she isn't half as bad as she is painted!'(9) In that typical, acid remark lay the fundamental difference between Mrs Greville and Lady Cunard – snobbism and intellect. She referred to Lady Cunard as 'The Lollipop' or the 'Yellow Canary' (a reference to her yellow hair and ubiquitous osprey-trimmed hats), while Lady Cunard retaliated by calling her 'The Discouri of Gloom'. As mistresses of formal and informal entertaining respectively, they epitomised the old and the new orders of Society.

The two women who were to dominate that informal style of entertaining of the twenties were Lady Cunard and Lady Colefax. Both were acknowledged as leading hostesses, a term that Lady Cunard loathed, once banning Cecil Beaton from her house and burning his *Book of Beauty* when she read that he had described her as such. They were, however, leaders of their sets for differing reasons and with wildly differing styles: Lady Cunard had the intellect, Lady Colefax had the energy, while Mrs Corrigan had the money. There were many other acknowledged hostesses who entertained a great deal, women like Mrs Somerset Maugham, the American Miss Elsa Maxwell and Madame Alfreda de Peña (who introduced the cocktail party to London in 1922), but they did not make a full-time 'career' out of cultivating the interesting, the influential or the Royal Family.

Of the three hostesses, Lady Cunard was in a league of her own. As her devoted, lifelong admirer George Moore described her, she was 'an artist, as much a social observer as La Rochefoucauld, or Madame de Sévigné, both of whom she admired. Her art lay in her conversation, that most evanescent form, and there was no Boswell to record it.'(10) Patrick Balfour (later Lord Kinross) thought her the one hostess in London worth cultivating, 'because at her house alone can you be sure of meeting interesting people and having fun into the bargain.'(11) Unlike Lady Colefax and Laura Corrigan, those whom she invited to lunch and to dine were there solely because they were interesting, never because they were grand or titled. Most of all, she had charm. She exuded goodwill, brightening the room and her guests. Roderick Cameron recalled that 'the moment she entered a room one was conscious of her presence. The diamond-like glitter of her wit was a tangible thing and she wore it like a jewel; it glowed round her like an aura round the moon, pale and phosphorescent, as exhilarating as the cold air of a frosty night.'(12)

She was as unlikely a hostess as she was successful. Born Maud (later she changed her name to Emerald) Burke from San Francisco, she married the immensely rich Sir Bache Cunard, grandson of the founder of the shipping line. It was an empty and ill-assorted marriage with only one child, Nancy. He was passionate about hunting and the country, she was well-read and highly intelligent, and it was no surprise to her friends or his when they separated sixteen years later. Lady Cunard left her husband in 1911 and went to live in London. For the next forty years she was to dominate London Society.

When the Asquiths moved into 10 Downing Street, Lady Cunard took their house at 20 Cavendish Square, but it was when she took the lease on a large house in Grosvenor Square that her *salon* really flourished. Chips Channon, unashamedly partisan, recalled the house as where

> the great met the gay, that statesmen consorted with Society, and writers with the rich – and where, for a year [1936] the drama of Edward VIII was enacted. It had a rococo atmosphere – the conversation in the candlelight, the elegance, the bibliots and the books: more, it was a rallying point for most of London society: only those who were too stupid to amuse the hostess, and so were not invited, were disdainful. The Court always frowned on so brilliant a *salon*, indeed Emerald's only failures were the two Queens and Lady Astor and Lady Derby. Everyone else flocked, if they had the chance. To some it was the most consummate bliss even to cross her threshold. She is as kind as she is witty, and her curious mind, and the lilt of wonder in her voice when she says something calculatedly absurd, are quite unique.(13)

The invitations to the three or four luncheon or dinner parties she gave each week usually came by telephone. More often than not the parties were organised just the day before. Unpunctuality was almost a disease for Lady Cunard, even for her own parties. Often guests unknown to each other had to struggle on their own for half an hour before the arrival of their hostess – an arrival, according to Harold Acton, 'always worth waiting for, a scented breeze of welcome.' She would often make some excuse in her husky voice, 'like a corncrake': 'My maid is furious with me – she says I am not properly dressed and she hasn't had time to straighten my eyelashes.'(14)

Once she had arrived in the drawing-room, Lady Cunard then introduced her guests, not that her introductions were of the slightest use to any of them. Some were related, others had known each other since childhood, and in any case the majority had been talking for the last half-hour. The introductions followed the train of her own whimsical thoughts – Lord Paramour, The Great Lover, or The Idealist. When she actually mentioned a guest's name, it was qualified with some flight of fancy. James Lees-Milne, then head of the National Trust, was introduced as 'the man who looks after all the public houses', and Lord Alington as the man who 'drives in a taxi at dawn from Paris to Rome, wearing evening dress and a gardenia, without any *luggage*'. Peter Hesketh was the 'man who owns a whole town'. Occasionally this frivolity went awry. Prince Youssupoff took great exception at being described as the 'man who murdered Rasputin', and left.

Once seated at the luncheon- or dinner-table, Lady Cunard dominated the scene she had created for that day. Harold Acton thought 'the conversation flowed like champagne' through her. She would introduce a topic of conversation and then, if her guests did not instantly respond or tackle it in a way which she approved, she would change the subject. The guests had to be quick to keep up with her changes. She was generally succinct and direct, guests hanging on her words as she led the conversation from the front. No one was allowed to be boring as she spirited the pompous away from their subjects. 'She made heavy politicians and financiers aware of another world beyond their ken and in a subtle way she influenced them and educated them.'(15) Nor was the conversation vulgar, for Lady Cunard had very clear definitions of what was and what was not permissible at her table. She liked, and provoked, dispute, but, unlike Mrs Greville, she would not stand for malicious gossip. One of her favourite ploys, however, was to tease the more opinionated of her guests. 'She would whizz round him like a humming bird till he became completely dizzy and he began to doubt his own identity.'(16) A typical example of a Cunard tease was directed against a corpulent American, Myron Taylor. When asked what he thought about incest, he began a somewhat laborious reply, so Lady Cunard immediately changed the subject to opera, singing the closing aria of Act I of *The Valkyrie*. When Mr Taylor droned on unperturbed by the interruption, Lady Cunard asked Kenneth Clark what he thought about incest. When he said that he was in favour of it, Lady Cunard's reply was, 'What a wicked thing to say, think of the Greeks', followed by a recitation of a passage from the *Oresteia*. Mr Taylor looked perplexed as Lady Cunard continued, 'But all the same it was just a silly old taboo, like Pythagoras saying that it was wicked to eat beans. Do you think that it is wicked to eat beans, Mr Taylor?'(17) By that time, Mr Taylor was thoroughly lost. No one was above her teasing and her wit. When Somerset Maugham, whom she admired, left one of her parties early with the excuse, 'I have to keep my youth', Lady Cunard replied, 'Then why didn't you bring him with you?'

After dinner was as enlightening as before, with a play-reading or a recital, the guests often being asked, and pleased, to

perform. Occasionally, one of the great contemporary compos-
ers, like Delius or Richard Strauss, would play one of his own
pieces. Like all her guests, Harold Acton found himself en-
tranced by these evenings,

> when nothing mattered but the purest art, whose essence
> was all round us like the fragrance of cassia . . . Lady
> Cunard had created an ideal setting for a synthesis of the
> arts. One could abandon onself joyfully, inhaling the
> luxuriance of sight and soul until one was lapped into
> silence. The pretentiousness that invaded the other
> 'literary' houses was absent: there was never a false
> note . . . Life at Grosvenor Square was thoroughly spent,
> not economised.(18)

Although outside the scope of this book, no reference to Lady
Cunard is complete without mention of her daughter, Nancy,
and her relationship with Sir Thomas Beecham. Her daughter
was her complete antithesis. While Lady Cunard declared that
'Motherhood is a low thing – the lowest' and was deeply
embarrassed by her daughter, Nancy loathed her mother, de-
claring to George Moore, 'I don't *like* her ladyship'. Once, playing a game of naming the person they would most like to see
come into the room, Nancy went so far as to reply, 'Lady Cunard
dead'. Her unrequited affair with Sir Thomas Beecham claimed
all of her heart and a great deal of her fortune.

While Lady Colefax did not have the breeding of Lady
Londonderry, the money of Mrs Greville or the patter of Lady
Cunard, she did have remarkable energy, a temperament strong
enough to withstand any rebuff or refusal, and a persistence that
astonished all. Where Mrs Greville pursued Royalty, Lady
Cunard only those who amused her, Sybil Colefax unashamedly
pursued anyone whom she considered remotely important,
although her address book was 'not compiled from Burke nor the
Almanach de Gotha; she was more drawn to *Who's Who* and
The Writers' and Artists' Year Book.'(19)

Lady Colefax, 'a kindly woman, well educated and well in-
formed, and a devoted wife and mother',(20) was quite genuinely
excited by talent in every shape or form, whether the talent was
literary, political, musical or artistic. But it was this unrelenting
lionising of the famous that prompted Osbert Sitwell to christen
her house, Argyll House in the King's Road, 'Lion's Corner
House', an apt title for one whose 'need to collect celebrities was
for her an addiction as strong as alcohol or drugs'.(21) She was
impressed by achievement rather than titles, which made her an
intellectual snob. Once she accepted an invitation to meet the

'P. of W.' – believing that she was to be introduced to the Prince of Wales – only to find that she was being teased and meeting a venerable clergyman, the Provost of Worcester. Although it was thought amusing to laugh at Lady Colefax behind her back (she was known quite openly as 'The Coalbox'), she did have a very genuine following of friends. Furthermore, a woman who is neither nobly born, rich, nor even good looking, does not create a brilliant *salon* with habitués of the calibre of Max Beerbohm, Desmond McCarthy, Duff Cooper, Lord Balfour and Lord Birkenhead without being in some way brilliant herself. No one of the stature of Virginia Woolf would have given her friendship, and a close friendship at that, if she were as inconsequential as she was painted. Having first thought her 'silly . . . hard, shiny and bright', Virginia Woolf came to recognise that she was a 'nice, good, discerning woman'.(22) She could spot talent in the young: before anybody else had heard of Noël Coward, Lady Colefax attended the first night of *The Vortex* in a draughty theatre in Hampstead. When she visited the dressing-room, the inevitable invitation to dine was given and a brilliant, lifelong friend made. Rising stars like John Gielgud, Ivor Novello, Rex Whistler, Harold Nicolson and Cecil Beaton were all caught young in the same way.

At the height of her social success throughout the twenties and early thirties, Lady Colefax was giving as many as six dinner or lunch parties a week. Argyll House was a perfect setting for entertaining. Set behind severe black railings and a paved courtyard, this red-brick, eighteenth-century house had beautifully proportioned rooms, and a large garden at the rear. Lady Colefax's taste was impeccable and she was to set a style that is still fashionable today – soft, muted colours, uncluttered rooms, the fabrics blending in with the rest of the room. Her immediate neighbours were Mrs Somerset Maugham (whose rooms by contrast were almost entirely white) and the music hall artist, Gwen Farrar.

The hallmark of Sybil Colefax's entertaining was her passion for writing invitation cards. Many hours each day were devoted to the writing of anything between thirty and fifty invitations in her near illegible hand. Despite the number, she rarely made the mistake of asking the wrong person for the wrong day. If there was somebody she really wanted, she would ask them again and again, her persistence gradually breaking down their resistance, until they accepted. Gerald Berners (who unexpectedly succeeded as Lord Berners 'when all three uncles fell off a bridge at the same time') unkindly adapted a Victorian toy he owned, a large japanned head of a blackamoor that stood in his hall, so that when a button was pressed, its mouth opened and out spewed dozens of unanswered invitations from Lady Colefax.

Like Lady Cunard's guests, Lady Colefax's were never dull. Lord Berners suggested that the only difference between the two women was that 'Sybil Colefax's evenings were a party of lunatics presided over by an efficient, trained hospital nurse, while Emerald Cunard's were a party of lunatics presided over by a lunatic'.(23) The only guaranteed bore at her parties, however, was her husband, Sir Arthur Colefax, of whom Lord Berners suggested that the Government had paid him £30,000 a year to bore the Channel Tunnel. Her guest lists were carefully worked out for the best mix of people. They could be very grand, from the Prince of Wales downwards; intellectual, such as W. B. Yeats, Virginia Woolf and E. F. Benson; political, like Winston Churchill and Austen Chamberlain; theatrical, like Lillian Braithwaite or Olga Lynn, the singer; or American, from Charlie Chaplin and Condé Nast to Mary Pickford and Thornton Wilder. Her list of friends and acquaintances, on both sides of the Atlantic, was formidable.

Whoever was present (save at the rare appearance of Royalty), lunch and dinner were both informal affairs with very much a family atmosphere. Compared to most women in London and certainly her rivals, her staff was minimal – Mrs Gray, the cook, Briance, the chauffeur, and Fielding, her devoted ladies' maid. Despite her comparative lack of servants and money, the quality of the food and the wine was excellent.

Conversation was led, some would say diverted, by Lady Colefax with her 'questing, restless brain' in a 'voice that seemed to echo through a silver sieve'.(24) She was extremely well read, especially in modern literature, although many thought that her views came from the pages of *The Times Literary Supplement*. What did characterise her conversation was the incessant torrent of Christian names,

> names of the great, the near great, and those who someday might be great – one hoped in the not too distant future. The Christian names dropped from her thin, pinkish lips like the rattle of ornaments on an overloaded bangle. 'Darling Virginia [Woolf]' – pointing to a copy of *The Waves*, prominently displayed on the table in the hall – 'insisted that I should read this before going to bed. But Arthur [Rubinstein] came to supper and began to play that enchanting piece of nonsense that Willie [Sir William Walton] had written for Osbert's [Sir Osbert Sitwell] *Façade*. So what is one to do?'(25)

She was also guilty of what became known as a 'colefaxismus' – to impress others by passing on details of the famous that only you are privy to. Margot Asquith once remarked, 'It is tiresome that Sybil is always on the spot. One can't talk about the birth of Christ without that Astrakhan ass saying she was there at the manger.'(26) Ronald Storrs deplored her habit of 'capping everything with a more celebrated but less well-fitting cap'.(27) Nevertheless, however maddening her interruptions must have been, however inconsequential her table, her guests continued to accept her invitations.

Later, money ran short through bad investments in America, and she had to move into a smaller house, in North Street, but she did not let up on her entertaining for a minute. Even when she started her interior decoration business, later to be joined by John Fowler to create Colefax and Fowler, she still found time to organise her endless round of dinners and luncheons. Her pursuit of celebrities eventually affected her health and, 'as though from the strain of constantly keeping her ear to the ground in the hope of catching their approaching footfalls, her body became increasingly bent'.(28) When she died in 1950, she was greatly missed. She genuinely loved people and putting them together; the lion-hunting in the end was just seen as harmless pastime.

While the individual characteristics of all these hostesses can so easily be contrasted, and in some cases were diametrically opposed, Mrs Laura Corrigan was an amalgam of all their better points. Like Lady Cunard, she was an American; she was as rich, if not richer, than Mrs Greville and also had her penchant for Royalty and the grand; she had the energy and persistence of Lady Colefax, as well as her kind and generous nature.

Mrs Laura Corrigan arrived in London in 1921 with the sole idea of entering Society. Her origins and the playboy image of her husband, Jimmy Corrigan, disqualified her from Cleveland Society (where the Corrigan steel fortune came from) and she was laughed out of New York Society as a pretentious and flashy upstart, nobody even bothering to find out what she was like. After a brief interlude in Paris, she presented herself to London Society, unannounced and totally unknown. Within two years, she was the talk of London, and invitations to her lavish parties were eagerly accepted – a success that lasted nearly twenty-five years.

Unlike the starchy New York Society, London Society has always had enough confidence to welcome into its ranks anyone who is thought to be entertaining, provided they behave properly and follow the rules. When Mrs Corrigan arrived in England, the self-indulgent London Society's sole aim in life was to have fun. Mrs Corrigan's style and generosity at least satisfied that aim. She also had two lucky breaks. The first came at a dinner given by a fellow American, the Countess of Stafford, where she learned that Mrs Alice Keppel, the friend of Edward VII, planned to live abroad and so let her house, 16 Grosvenor Street.

Mrs Corrigan took the beautiful house furnished. With the furniture came Mr and Mrs Rolfe, he a butler of the highest pre-war standards, she a cook of exceptional quality, and a full staff of twenty indoor servants. A further fee was negotiated by Mrs Keppel to leave her visitors' book behind. The second break came when Rolfe, who had started by plucking surprised friends of Mrs Keppel's off the street to meet Mrs Corrigan, suggested that she should contact Charlie Stirling, Lady Londonderry's ex-private secretary.

Charlie Stirling was a splendid success and, with an exorbitant financial inducement, completely took her over. 'Professor Higgins' advised her whom to invite and when, what to serve and to say, and how to dress and behave at all times, both as a guest and a hostess. Thus primed, she entered Society at one of the highest levels by accepting an invitation (cleverly arranged by Stirling in return for a charitable contribution) from Lady Londonderry herself. The two women liked each other instantly – Lady Londonderry recognising the undoubted courage shown by Mrs Corrigan in entering her world, Mrs Corrigan happy to be there at all. Once the Marquess and his wife accepted the return invitation to dine, Mrs Corrigan was in, and instantly became *the* object of curiosity for London Society.

To the younger and more impecunious members of Society, Laura Corrigan was a godsend – they accepted her invitations gladly as they knew that they would be able to gossip with all their friends (Charlie Stirling had seen to that), eat superb food, drink her exceptional champagne and dance – all at her expense. In return, Mrs Corrigan simply delighted in having them as her guests. It did not matter that they regarded her as a joke – her malapropisms and sayings were soon to become the talk of London. Mrs Keppel's chairs were spoilt by the *petits pois* on the seats; her house in London was her *ventre à terre*; her reply to the ballet dancers she had hired for a cabaret who had suggested that they should perform Debussy's *Prélude à l'Après-midi d'un Faune* was 'Oh my! what do I want with a ballet about a telephone?'(29) In addition to her *faux pas*, her appearance also excited comment. She had had her eyes operated on to make them wider, and they failed to close even when she slept. She also wore a wig – as a result of some childhood illness that had left her completely bald. As Daphne Vivian recalled:

It was an open secret that Laura Corrigan wore a wig. She owned several, all in a peculiar bright shade of auburn but each appropriately designed for its own specific purpose and occasion – perfectly groomed, for luncheon or dinner in London; slightly rumpled, for breakfast in bed; wind-blown, for week-ends in the country; more than ordinarily dishevelled, for visits to a notional *coiffeur*; with a bathing-cap attached, for swimming. (I actually saw that latter come off one day when she dived into the sea from a yacht. The sight of a head like a knee appearing on the surface would have been a dreadful embarrassment, but she avoided this by stoically remaining under water until she had retrieved it and redonned her head-gear.) The most important item of her luggage was a large leather case in which these wigs of hers were transported. Its contents were as intriguing to us as those of Pandora's box, but none of us ever dared to open 'Laura's wigwam'.(30)
The *Sunday Express* even dubbed her 'The Big Wig of London'.

By her fourth season, Laura Corrigan was well established as a leading hostess of a glittering, but somewhat unintellectual, section of Society. Lady Cunard, more as a tease than a kindness, sat her next to George Moore at lunch. When Moore observed, 'I always think, Mrs Corrigan, that of all the sexual perversions, chastity is the most incomprehensible,' she could only reply, 'I guess I'll have to think that one over, Mr Moore.'(31)

It was not long before she was sure enough of herself and her position in Society to dispense with the services of Charlie Stirling. Only occasionally did she make a 'social gaffe' – once she placed 'Jubie' Lancaster (born on Queen Victoria's Jubilee Day, he was known as Jubie all his life) as if he were the Duke of Lancaster. She did, however, overcome the situation by shouting out, 'Hands up the next ranking Dook!'(32) It was no wonder that Laura Corrigan and her parties were so popular. Each one was carefully worked out, with military precision, and costed down to the last pound. It was nothing for her to spend £6,000 on a party. Her décor was lavish and exciting – the garden would be transformed into a ballroom just for the night, with singers dressed as statues to entertain the guests. For one party, in July 1924, she transformed the house into *'le jardin des perroquets verts'*; for another, she had the curtains sprayed with powdered glass then carefully lit, so that they sparkled. Often, these were 'surprise parties', with the invitations going out at the last minute – news of a lavish Corrigan party could never be kept a secret.

She spent fortunes giving her guests ridiculously expensive

presents. Each guest drew a number from a tombola and it was a well known 'secret' that the draw was rigged – the most expensive 'prizes' going to the grandest people (once Michael Hornby received a gold cigarette case ear-marked for Prince George). Initially the tombola was a form of bribe to tempt the guests she most wanted to come. Daphne Fielding remembered that

> the magnificence of the prizes offered at her cotillions proved to be ample bait and in a short time all the big fish were hooked – dukes by coroneted gold sock suspenders, the lesser fry by initialled braces with solid tabs, fashionable brides by pink monogrammed sheets and, in due course, rattles with gold bells for their offspring. I myself was delighted to receive a comb of gold and tortoiseshell in a pink leather Cartier case, the first I had ever seen.(33)

There was always a night-club atmosphere about her parties. She was the first hostess to include a cabaret at her dances, either with professional singers or acrobats, or just using her guests. One memorable night, 21 July 1926, the evening's cabaret was:

> *On the ukele* . . . Lady Louis Mountbatten singing a plantation number accompanied by Lady Brecknock and Mrs Richard Norton
> *Exhibition dance* . . . Lady Plunket
> *Double tandem cycle act* . . . Daphne Vivian and Lord Weymouth, with Lady Lettice Lygon and Lord Brecknock singing 'Daisy, Daisy'
> *A satire* . . . Lady Loughborough and Poppy Baring
> *A duet* . . . Michael Hornby and Bobby Jenkinson

The finale of that party was provided by the hostess herself who, with enormous verve, danced the Charleston in a top hat and red shoes. She then demonstrated her penchant for standing on her head, first taking the precaution of tying a scarf round her skirt. Lady Maud Warrender, daughter of the Earl of Shaftesbury, had to be restrained from doing her plate breaking act for fear of damaging the parquet floor. The party was a great success and ended with a game of 'the disappearing aristocrat', where the guests just melted away at four a.m.

Apart from the year her husband died, 1928, Laura Corrigan came to London every year, giving her famous parties. When Mrs Keppel's house was sold, she took a succession of houses, among them Crewe House, the Duke of Marlborough's house in

Kensington Palace Gardens, and Dudley House in Park Lane, which cost her £5,000 for two months. David Herbert remarked that he never heard her say anything interesting, she had no humour and she was undeniably an appalling snob. Yet, she was kind and generous, to a fault, and immensely popular for herself, rather than her millions. When Laura Corrigan, the daughter of a lumberjack, died in 1946, her memorial service was attended by 'Royalty, ambassadors, peers and peeresses of the highest rank, a churchful of people who had been fond of her and amused by her.'(34)

9

THE GENERATION GAP

'Si la Vieillesse Pouvait, Kitty'

*T*HE EFFECT OF THE FIRST
World War on the young was to be lasting and dramatic, particularly among the young men who had come to manhood in the twenties, and had thus been too young to fight. They entered a world of insecurity, yet their education at public schools and universities equipped them solely for the secure, moneyed life of a gentleman of leisure. Even at home, many parents passed on their 'mantle of Edwardian materialism and totally hedonistic attitude'(1) to their children, although the times and the system in which they had been brought up had changed so drastically. So they became hybrids, hovering between two worlds.

Also, many younger sons lived in the shadow of elder brothers killed in the war, with the inevitable, invidious comparisons. In Society, the 'boys who had died' had had all the advantages, and disadvantages, of wealth and position. They had lived a life of gentlemanly ease with a firm belief in the excellence and permanence of their world. In 1914, war was still an intrinsically noble tradition, and the education and the traditions of upbringing of those who went so happily to the front, ideally fitted them to become romantic war heroes. Without wishing to disparage their heroism, it is true say that those 'who made the supreme sacrifice' were often endowed retrospectively with superlative qualities which they may, or equally may not, have possessed – Lady Marchmain's three brothers, who were killed in the war between Mons and Passchendaele, were 'always perfect' in her eyes, even though Ned, 'the eldest of three legendary heroes', was once imprisoned 'for taking a bear into one of Lloyd George's meetings'.(2). Either way, the slain brother was 'a hard act to follow', held up as a shining example to his younger brothers. Those younger brothers who were urged to be worthy of such paragons were the first to turn to defiant frivolity: why take life seriously when it could so easily be slaughtered in the mud of another Flanders field? It was no wonder that they were cynical, or that they turned out as they did, either deeply introverted or wildly extrovert.

The generation chasm between parents and their sons in the 1920s was wider than ever before. Traditionally, the young are either led by, or compete with, their elder brothers or skip a generation and consult their grandparents. In the main, post-war young men had no elder brothers to guide them and their grandparents were pure Victorians, products of a bygone age. Their parents would not deviate from their preconceived beliefs. For them, it was unthinkable that their sons should not have the same education as their grandfathers. After that, it was left to them to carve out for themselves as marked and profitable a career as possible, despite the qualifications and tastes engendered by that education and the shortage of money handed out by their parents. It was not surprising that these post-war young men rebelled; they rebelled against parental tyranny and the limited conception of life for which it stood, but still without a constructive policy. They were a confused generation; 'planted in one soil, they found themselves of a sudden growing in another; and so their growth was arrested. Too fastidious for the new world, their roots were yet no longer planted in the old. They were intermediates, like the creatures in Barrie's Never-Never Land who did not quite know *what* they were.'(3)

In 1925, the *Daily Express* came out with a bitter attack on 'The Modern Girl's Brother'. He was cited as being 'weary, anaemic, feminine, bloodless, dolled up like a girl, an exquisite without masculinity and resembling a silken-coated lapdog', but the article qualified these epithets with the assurance that 'it is not suggested that he is sexually depraved'.(4)

Compared to the post-war young men, the change in the fortunes of the 'Modern Woman' was infinitely better, but still not without its problems. On the whole, she had benefitted by the war, which had given her a taste of independence. Before the war, suffragettes had chained themselves to railings, gone to prison and made a great deal of noise in their campaign to secure the vote, but the part that women played in the war, such as the girls in munitions factories or nurses at the Russian front, had a far greater effect on their eventual emancipation. Women who were over thirty and householders (or married to one) were given the vote in 1919, although it was an anomaly that they could also, like Lady Astor, be Members of Parliament at twenty-one. It was not until 1927 that women over the age of twenty-one were given what the *Daily Sketch* called the 'Girls' Eastertide Gift'(5) by the Prime Minister, Stanley Baldwin. Conservative papers dubbed it the 'flapper vote'.

In the late nineteenth century, a flapper had been a child prostitute, and later the term had been modified and refined during the war to describe 'a young girl with a long pigtail and a large bow at the back. She was not grown up so could go out with young men without being compromised.'(6) In the twenties, the description was modified again to mean any girl with a boyish figure. 'Flapperism' had begun in Germany, where those girls were known as *backfisch*. It was considered a 'sexual reaction against over-fed women, under-exercised monumental women, and as a compromise between pederasty [with their boyish figures] and normal sex.'(7) During the war, the shortages of butter and sugar and the popularity of tennis and other games had generally reduced girls' weight; when they were 'freed' of their old-fashioned corsets, the hour-glass figure became almost cylindrical, and with the new shape came a freedom in clothes and outlook. Later, a flapper became any modern, independent girl with a zest for life. She smoked in public and drank cocktails. She affected a Cockney accent and phrases at will. Nina Blount, the archetypal flapper in *Vile Bodies*, when asked if she minded being seduced, replied: 'Not as much as all that,' . . . and added in Cockney, 'Charmed I'm sure.'(8) They talked endlessley about sex, with a casualness which might or might not be genuine: '"Hello darling, how's your sex-life?" "Lousy, how's yours?"'(9) was a fashionable greeting of the time. The flapper had the latch key to her home.

Every generation believes that it has invented sex but, 'by and large, no age is naughtier than any other; the sexual impulse is as regular and rhythmical as the surge of the tides; its ripples and variations are merely a kind of social spray, dependent upon external circumstances'.(10) Beverley Nichols believed that in the twenties, that reputation for 'naughtiness' was largely 'conceived with printers' ink and moulded with the compositors' fingers'. What promiscuity there was in Society was at least conducted discreetly (Nichols going so far as to say that it was carried on 'with elegance and refinement')(11).

During the war, sexual conventions were needfully relaxed. The flapper and the subaltern had their affairs, but it was consciously reckless. It was a lark, rather than a revolt; it defied the rules with the excuse of the emergency. When the war ended, it was thought that 'young people would settle down to obey, so far as the flesh allowed, the good old Victorian precepts.'(12) Such thinking might have been justified, but for various changes in the post-war moral equation.

'The simple process of dissociating sex-life from the philoprogenitive instinct was performed by the War Generation,' laboriously intoned Richard Aldington. For the first time, advice on contraception was available to everyone. In one stroke, Dr Marie Stopes' manual on *Married Love* abolished the major risk of unmarried love: 'free love' for the first time really was free. The feminist movement accelerated after 1918. Before the war, the feminist was not quite feminine; after the war women became feminist by compulsion. No longer would they tolerate the double standard of morality, where men were allowed, even encouraged, to sow the traditional wild oats while women were not – unless, of course, they belonged to that 'specialised outcast group that had to exist to make the wild oat system workable'.(13) To make the double standard into a single standard, either the man's activities were to be curtailed or the women's freedom expanded. Gradually, the latter process took place. 'After the war, the mothers and the aunts dragged the morals of their daughters back to their own prim day, but as the decade progressed, so the morals got looser and looser. By 1925, it was exceptional if an unmarried girl slept with a man: during the thirties, it was quite the norm, it had merely ceased being hushed up.'(14)

To some women, marriage was the ticket to promiscuity. The same women who would not blink at the idea of having an affair after marriage, especially in the hunting world, would have been horrified at the idea before: *vide* Charles Ryder and Lady Julia Flyte in *Brideshead*. Many men simply found married women more 'convenient' than single girls.

There was still a certain stigma attached to divorce, despite the fact that a twenties divorce was a complete charade. Whereas a husband only needed to prove adultery by his wife, she had to prove cruelty or desertion by her husband, as well as adultery, to gain her divorce. In practice, however, it was the husband who 'did the gentlemanly thing', supplying the evidence of adultery by spending 'a blameless night' with a 'woman unknown' in an hotel, all fixed by his solicitor, a scene so accurately and wittily portrayed by Evelyn Waugh in *A Handful of Dust*. The more salacious details of the evidence were reported in the Press until restrained by the Judicial Proceedings (Regulation of Reports) Act, 1926.

Obviously, such sexual freedom had its critics, notably the Church, the Home Secretary, Sir William Joynson-Hicks (later Lord Brentford), nicknamed 'Jix', and, hypocritically, certain elements of the Press. Newspapers referred to syphilis as 'a certain disease'; rape was 'a certain suggestion'; and the result of that certain suggestion left the woman in 'a certain condition'. Outside 'certain circles', homosexuality was unthinkable. On hearing that Lord Beauchamp was a homosexual, George V is said to have muttered, 'I thought people like that shot themselves'. Like-minded hearties threw Cecil Beaton into the river at Lord Herbert's twenty-first birthday ball at Wilton House.

'Homosexuality had been on the increase among the upper classes for a couple of generations, although almost unknown among working people.'(15) Amongst boys, it was especially fostered by the public school boarding system. At university and post university, homosexuals 'melted' into Society, which was, as ever, ready to be entertained and seduced by charm, the hallmark of those overt homosexuals, men like Noël Coward, Oliver Messel and Cecil Beaton. To quote the popular song, homosexuals may be headaches, but they are seldom bores.

Lesbians were quieter about their aberrations, but could easily justify themselves, if called upon to do so, by pointing out that there were not enough men to go around. The majority of the public had never even heard of a lesbian until the trial of *The Well of Loneliness*, the novel by Miss Radcliffe Hall. It was a monstrous case, brought after the book was condemned in an article by James Douglas, who wrote of it: 'I would rather give a healthy boy or girl a phial of prussic acid than this novel.' The only 'offending' sentence that Beverley Nichols could find in the whole book was: 'That night they [the two women] were not divided'.

For generations, Society has always accepted both heterosexuals and homosexuals alike, so long as there was no scandal. Those of the previous, and later, generations who decried the twenties as licentious, were hypocrites. Often, such condemnation by the older generation was born out of simple jealousy, as with the two mothers in *Vile Bodies* discussing what the young *do* at parties:

'Oh to be young again, Kitty. When I think, my dear, of all the trouble and exertion which we had to go through to be

moderately bad . . . those passages in the early morning and mama sleeping next door.'
'And yet my dear, I doubt very much whether they really *appreciate* it all as much as we should . . . young people take things so much for granted. *Si la jeunesse savait.'*
'*Si la vieillesse pouvait*, Kitty.'(16)

In any age, women's fashions tend to be a yard-stick as to their current thinking. In the 1920s, their fashion represented the spirit of their new-found emancipation. A figure was something to be ashamed of: 'the unforgivable sin against smartness this spring [1921] is to have a figure . . . the modern *élégante's* frocks are streamlined as severely as a racing car.'(17) *Punch*, took it further: stating that figures were hopelessly out of fashion and 'the sweet slinky' look was admired. They reported the apocryphal story that 'A London Society woman has a pet snake. We doubt, however, if the fashion will spread, as most women are inclined to be jealous of snakes because they have no hips.'(18) Women worked hard to achieve their figures and to keep them – 'reducing salts', Hollywood diets, massage, 'a daily dozen' of gymnastic exercises and a clever dressmaker were all that was needed for the perfect 'schoolboy figure'. If nature failed a woman, there were always artificial means. According to Beverley Nichols, 'It was the battle of the brassière in reverse; and half the dressmaker's time was spent in making intricate contraptions of canvas and elastic to be fitted over any bust that showed signs of intransigence. To own a bust in the twenties, was extremely *déclassé.'*(19)

Another typical outward 'badge' of women's emancipation in the twenties was the jumper. Jumpers were a product of the knitting habit in the war – after the whole population had finished creating 'enough mufflers to strangle half a dozen armies',(20) women took to knitting jerseys for themselves. They were generally V-necked, loose, shapeless and long enough to cover the hips. Although the jumper did not come in for men until 1923, some even following the Prince of Wales and his series of Fair Isle golfing sweaters, first seen when he 'drove himself in' as captain of the Royal and Ancient Golf Club at St Andrews, they at least symbolised a bi-sexual garment. One husband was to complain vociferously at the jumper he was expected to wear: 'half squares and crosses and half circles and rhomboids and blobs, crawled and twisted and intertwined in intricate confusion, dazzling devastating colours and Shetland floss wool.'(21)

Over these boyish figures (for a man to refer to a woman as

'boyish' was the highest compliment he could pay her), raged the 'Great Skirt Controversy'. In 1920, the hem of day-time dresses plummeted even lower than the pre-war level, but rose steadily to above the knee after 1923. Beverley Nichols was quick to condemn the exposure of the knee:

> There is nothing, but nothing, to be said for the female knee. It is the one part of the female anatomy that has left the poets cold since the days of Sappho. Ears, yes, and necks and eyes and ankles and nostrils and teeth and chins and fingernails and even toes . . . all these have been celebrated. But when confronted by that small patch of skin which conceals the semi-lunar cartilage, the poets have always been struck dumb. Not until the twenties did the knee come into its own.(22)

The knee was, of course, covered by stockings. The decade that introduced the shortest skirts in the history of fashion, also produced the ugliest stockings to go with them. Silk stockings were introduced at the end of the war, but soon became scarce and therefore expensive. The smartest stockings had clocks, either embroidered or in open latticework, and were generally black. By 1921, the artificial silk stocking had arrived and came in new colours: besides black there was white, nigger (an acceptable term for dark brown), toney (a reddish brown peculiar to the twenties), and the ubiquitous beige. Beige was everywhere – when the Society hostess Lady Mendl first saw the Parthenon, she declared in rapture, 'My favourite colour, beige!' Beverley Nichols recalled the first time he saw beige stockings at the Ritz in the summer of 1922 on the two young Trix sisters, 'and a number of elderly ladies felt that the country had taken another step towards the pit. Beige suggested the nude, and the nude – then as now – was not quite nice.'(23)

Nor were such masculine colours confined to stockings. Dresses appeared in a variety of unattractive colours: tango orange, cerise and the predominant colour, green. Michael Arlen describes a scene in a night-club, supposedly based on the Embassy Club: 'There were many green dresses: jade green, October green, rusty green, soft green, sea green, dying green, and shades of green that would suit the expiring voices of formal women in a garden by Watteau. There were thirty-nine green dresses. There was a Jewess of the wrong sort in the wrong sort of green. She looked like a fat asparagus.'(24) Even Edith Sitwell had 'jade green moods':

Jade-green my mood today, C minor,
The only tea I drink is China.

Punch cited a man attempting to buy a 'dainty scarf in a pretty colour' only to be told by the shop assistant that they came in 'all the new shades: Mud, Nigger, Rust, Gunmetal, Old Boots, Dust and Self.'(25)

So flimsy were women's clothes by 1926 that one fashion article announced that 'a woman can be fully dressed this summer and have thirty ounces of clothing, and this included an allowance of sixteen ounces for the shoes.' The excitement of such scant attire – 'a one-piece under-garment, a one-piece over-garment that barely reaches the knees, a slender belt for stocking-suspenders, shoes and stockings' – prompted a Mr Corbett-Smith to write:

> One notable businessman of my acquaintance told me that he had to abandon travelling to town by tube or bus, taking a taxi instead. He found it quite impossible to sit opposite to those young women. One of the most distinguished lawyers in the City of London told me that when his young daughter brought her girl-friends down to his house for dinner and they curled up in arm-chairs he was inevitably driven to take refuge in the billiard-room. The provocation of silken leg and half naked thigh, together with little or no concealment of the breasts, was devastating and over-whelming.(26)

Total condemnation and fury, rather than lust, was more the norm. The older generation, particularly the Church, was vehement in its criticism of women's fashions. Father Bernard Vaughan began with 'Today's fashions are designed not to drape the human form and keep it warm, beautiful and comfortable, but to awaken in man unholy desires.' The Pope ordered his Bishops to denounce them as scandalous. Viscountess Templeton described 'the outrageous dress' in the *Weekly Dispatch*, stating that it 'threatened devolution of the civilised woman of the twentieth century into the savage of unmemorial ages . . . the fashion of a certain class is rapidly returning to barbarism.' She went on to cite an army officer who did not dance at a ball as he 'could not ask any of the women; they had not got enough on.' She was joined by many others. The Duchess of Somerset maintained that 'the nude in sculpture suffices'; The Marchioness of Townshend found modern dress 'immoral in its inadequacy'.

Modern fashion, however, did have its supporters, often from surprising quarters. Mrs Stanley Baldwin said that 'as life depends of the liver [sic] so does the wearing of dress depend on the wearer. A nice girl can wear anything and yet look nice; an unpleasant one even in a nun's robe remains unpleasant. Personally, I do not go through life with disapproval in my eye and seeking where to place it.'(27)

In a footnote to a *Punch* cartoon in 1926, a Society woman introduces a girl to a visitor: 'You haven't met my niece, have you? She's quite a dear but a trifle old-fashioned. Men have to speculate as to her knees and ears.'(28) The hostess was referring to the length of her skirt and to her unfashionably long hair. Women had cut their hair during the war for purely practical reasons, whether for work or, as with the rich, owing to the lack of ladies' maids to manage it for them; it was even suggested that the only contribution that some women made to the war effort was to cut their hair. They grew it again hair soon after. When permanent waving arrived from America in 1922, short hair could be given a sophisticated look and 'bobbing' was in. Loelia Ponsonby recalled that 'permanent waving was a fairly new process and was as painful as going to the dentist. Sometimes it did not even work and one emerged with straighter hair than when one started.'(29)

After bobbing, women wore 'little pseudo-Greek buns which were hard to keep tidy. Much of the time, they were as towsled as beatniks.'(30) That was followed by shingling, the hair-style described by Michael Arlen, as worn by Iris Storm, the heroine of his novel *The Green Hat*:

> Her hair was thick and tawny and it waved like music, and the night was tangled in the waves of her hair. It was like a boy's hair, swept back from the forehead, which was a wide clear forehead, clean and brave and sensible as a boy's . . . Above her neck, her hair died a very manly death, a more manly death than 'bobbed' hair was ever known to die, and it comes about that Iris Storm was the first Englishwoman I ever saw with 'shingled' hair. This was in 1922.(31)

Other variations of short hair followed, including the 'Eton Bob' and the 'bingle'; 'you've bungled my bingle!' was a common cry to hairdressers. As with the short skirts, there were strong critics of the new coiffures. To many of the older generation short hair was the mark of the 'modern woman' and that was the sign of the devil. Beverley Nichols wrote of the mass of impassioned prose presented against the two hair-styles, 'One would think that "bobbing" and "shingling" were pseudonyms for Sodom and Gomorrah'.(32) Daphne Vivian's father forbade her to shingle her hair, believing 'a woman's hair is her crowning glory'. When he discovered that she had cut her hair, 'he flew into the blackest of baronial baits. He announced that he was not going to speak to me for a month, and I was not to pour out his breakfast coffee.'(33)

Lady Bland-Smith made a name for herself by announcing that girls with bobbed or shingled hair greatly reduced their chances of marriage, while a report appeared in *The Weekly Dispatch* that 'shingling, according to every medical man who had discussed the matter, though not unhealthy, is bound to make women, sooner or later, as bald as men.'(34) As with the short skirt, cropped hair was out by the end of the decade. It even became a fashionable act for a girl to be growing her hair, as *Punch*, in its pithy vein, commented:

First Young Woman of Fashion: My dear, you've had your hair cut off again!

Second Ditto: Yes, I have. Surely you know that it's only fashionable to be growing it?(35)

Along with the bobbed heads went the vogue for the cloche hat. As the hat had to be pulled down right over the eyebrows to be chic, it could only be comfortably worn with short hair. The cloche remained fashionable for several years, being worn lower and lower over the eyes to make the wearer unrecognisable. Such flying helmet-like hats had names like 'Crusader', 'Aviator' or 'Lindbergh' – after Charles Lindbergh had flown the Atlantic single-handed.

While women's fashions remained predominently masculine up to 1927, when a few frills appeared and the hem-line dropped, men's fashions, as far as they went, veered towards the feminine. Just as women took to the Eton Bob – one masculine girl complained that when she had her hair cut in a barber's shop it cost sixpence [2½p], but that the same thing cost 3/6d [17½p] when called an Eton Bob in a woman's hairdressers – men's hair was worn much longer. Some fops even went to Deauville to have their hair cut. There was a school of thought that the Oxford Bags were no more than pseudo-skirts. After appearing in Oxford (Cambridge would have it that they preceded Oxford by at least two years) they were copied by the East End tailors, and within a few weeks London was full of Oxford Bags, worn by young men whose Alma Mater was Oxford Street.

The new trousers billowed round the wearers' legs in incredible amplitude, and the flannel drapery trailed on the ground, hiding the feet. Strange dyes had transformed the conventional steel-grey; these trousers were fawn, or silver, or delicately pink or mauve. Where the accepted width of the trouser leg was seventeen inches at the knee and fifteen inches at the ankle, the corresponding measurement of these Oxford Bags was twenty-six and twenty-four inches.(36)

The new proportions in trousers even 'invaded' the dinner jacket and evenin. In London, as in the country, men always changed into black tie for dinner at home and white tie if they went out to dine, or went to the theatre or Covent Garden. Towards the end of the decade, soft shirts replaced the stiff-fronted shirts worn with dinner jackets. The fashion might not have been acceptable had not the Prince of Wales and his younger brother, the Duke of Kent, been seen wearing them. Evening dress, once so formal and unalterable, also changed. 'Figured white ties and waistcoats matched shirts; collars spread their wings and bows expanded like starched butterflies.'(37)
Like men's evening dress, their day-time clothes changed too. The narrow trousers, high buttoning jackets and stiff collars were slowly replaced by double-breasted suits with a 'lounge lizard' cut – square shouldered and waisted – and pale double-breasted waistcoats with lapels, worn under a single-breasted suit with wide trousers pleated at the waist, 'exquisitely reminiscent of the 1830s'. George V had two sartorial tastes, single-breasted suits and creasing his trousers down the seams; the former caught on, the latter, a Naval trait, did not.
The King wore a beard for most of his adult life, a fashion still common after the war. The sudden craze for 'Beaver' made the hirsuit take to the razor. 'Beaver' was a game played by two people walking down the street. The first to see a beard shouted 'beaver' and scored a point; a white beard, known as a 'polar-beaver', scored more. The first to twenty points was the winner. The cry certainly made the beard unfashionable, so much so that by 1924 the King, 'distinguished foreigners, and a few Chelsea Pensioners were for some years almost the only bearded men left in Great Britain'.(38) These taunts were good-natured, and although they sounded rude, there was no malice.

10

DANCE, DANCE, DANCE

'Nights in the Jazz Jungle'

$\mathcal{W}$HEN THE AMERICAN TROOPS finally sailed back to the United States at the end of the war, they returned with the envy of the British, and a feeling of resentment against them for their exaggerated claims for their part in the war. They left behind, however, a more lasting legacy of gaiety, fashion, music, dancing, drink and fun; a legacy that was to become the hallmark of the 1920s. London was slowly transformed from the wartime aspect of 'dimmed street-lights, the carefully blinded windows, the rather neglected streets, the comparative absence of traffic and the air of being closed down indefinitely',[1] and once again became 'the centre of all that was new and exciting.

Immediately after the war, men and women of all classes had money to spend and were full of nervous energy. Their outlet for both was to dance, and they kept dancing for the decade. First they took to jazz, described by The *Daily Mail* as: 'This Jazz Age [where] people are dancing as they have never danced before, in a happy rebound from the austerities of war . . . But the dancing is not quite what it was in the dim old years before 1914.'[2] Syncopated music had been introduced from America before the war but had then been 'denounced as barbarous and blatant'.[3]

'Rag-time' was a pejorative term; a rag-time regiment was disorderly and untrustworthy. After the war, jazz and all the dance steps that went with it became 'all the rage'.

Opposition to such music and wild dancing was strong. Articles appeared in the Press. One, entitled 'Nights in the Jazz Jungle', denounced the dancing craze as 'spiritually, as well as literally, a case of the jumps'.(4) The jazz bands of the early 1920s were raucus, pumping out a relentless rhythm with drums, rattles, bells, hooters, whistles and banjoes; the more melodious saxophone and trumpet came in later.

New dances came and went quickly. Dances were given ridiculous names: the Twinkle, the Jog Trot, the Vampire, the Missouri Walk, the Hesitation, the Elfreda and the Camel Walk all had their day. In 1922, the fox-trot was *the* dance: Dr C. E. M. Joad, the noted radio panellist, recalled that 'you shuffled round the room in what a contemporary wit called "a form of country walking slightly impeded by a member of the opposite sex", and you called it a fox-trot. You slid round a little faster and called it a one-step . . . eventually the fox-trot and the one-step merged into a uniform shuffle which presented no difficulty to anybody.'(5)

The following year, the dancing mania was as much alive as ever, although the pace had slowed down, almost to a standstill. The music was melancholy, the dancing dreary and joyless. *Punch* captioned a cartoon of an American watching the dancing in a restaurant: 'Gee, wouldn't the *Marche Funèbre* make just the cutest one-step!'(6) By the end of 1923, the Blues had arrived. Michael Arlen in his novel, *The Green Hat*, described the new mood:

> We watched our elders dance with each other's mothers, and for them the band on the balcony played with a sensibility approaching grief. There was no tune. But it is absurd, this querulous demand of young people for 'tunes'! Our fathers and mothers have done with 'tunes'. Let there, our uncles say, be a rhythm. Let there, say our aunts, be syncopation. Grave, profound, unforgettable, there was a rhythm. It had a beat like the throb of an agonised heart lost in the artery of the Underground. Dolorous it was, yet phantasms of gaiety lay entwined in it . . . It reminded you of past and passing things. It reminded you of the days when people over forty had still enough restraint not to crowd out every ballroom and night-club with their dancing in open formation . . . You mourned the presence of the dead. You mourned the memory of the living. They call this rhythm the Blues.(7)

The sinuous movement of the Blues did not last long either, and was superseded in 1926 by the 'jumps and jerks' of the Charleston. As with all new dances, there was great competition to excel, the young and middle-aged going for lessons. Daphne Vivian recalled when

the Charleston and the Black Bottom had just been introduced into England. Brian [Howard] decided that we should all become proficient in the steps of these dances, and encouraged us all to take lessons in London from Barbara Back, the wife of a Harley Street surgeon. Michael Rosse became an expert and he and his sister, Bridget Parsons, caused surprise and envy in London ballrooms as together they danced a furious Charleston, both with a look of earnest concentration.

When Michael was at home at Birr Castle, he used to lock himself up in his rooms for hours, turn on the gramophone and practise his dancing. If he was in a bad mood he would Charleston so frantically to drive out the evil humour that the ceiling in the sitting-room below shook and quivered. (8)

For Society, the dancing mania was generally confined to their own houses, either at balls in London during the Season or in the country. They danced to wind-up gramophones, or to the wireless, from which they were invited to 'roll back the carpet . . . and take a few steps'. Even at Buckingham Palace, the Princess Royal gave impromptu *thés dansants* for her friends – at one such party, her brother, the then Prince Albert, remet the Lady Elizabeth Bowes-Lyon.

It was not until some of the licensing restrictions of the wartime DORA (Defence of the Realm Act) had been relaxed in 1921 that 'the restaurant habit' caught on. Although the shortage of servants at home contributed to people dining out more often, it was the dancing mania that drove them first to the restaurants, then to the new crop of night-clubs that sprang up all over London.

The Savoy Hotel started the fashion of dancing with meals, a fashion that was swiftly followed by every other restaurant and hotel. The food was generally of little importance; only the band, the music and the dance-floor mattered. Some hotels provided a cabaret as well:

After the theatre, one could go on to such places as the Hotel Metropole for the *Midnight Follies*, the Piccadilly Hotel for the *Piccadilly Revels*, the Savoy, the Trocadero, Princes, etc., where first-rate showmen of the calibre of

Charles B. Cochran and André Charlot presented supper entertainments with stars of such quality as Beatrice Lillie, Alice Delycia, Sophie Tucker, Jack Buchanan, the Trix sisters, Grock and Jack Hylton's band.(9)

Such establishments were totally respectable and kept within the law, and for their patrons such entertainment sufficed. For those who wanted more, the rich, who dined late, and the young, in their constant search for pleasure, there was the night-club. Some of them were respectable, but the majority were not. The police made no distinction between the eminently reputable night-clubs of Bond Street and the 'gilded night-spots' of Soho. Of the latter, Mrs Meyrick was the queen.

Mrs Kate Meyrick is thinly disguised in *Brideshead* as Ma Mayfield, whose club, the Old Hundredth in Sink Street, Soho, was probably 'The 400' which, although not owned by Mrs Meyrick, was identical to all her many other establishments.

'Members?' said the commissionaire.

'The name is Mulcaster,' said Mulcaster. 'Viscount Mulcaster.'

'Well, try inside,' said the commissionaire . . .

Inside the dark doorway was a bright hatch.

'Members?' asked a stout woman, in evening dress.

'I like that,' said Mulcaster, 'you ought to know me by now.'

'Yes, dearie,' said the woman without interest. 'Ten bob each.'

'Oh look here, I've never paid before.'

'Dare say not, dearie. We're full up tonight so it's ten bob. Anyone who comes after you will have to pay a quid. You're lucky.'

'Let me speak to Mrs Mayfield.'

'I am Mrs Mayfield.'

'Why, Ma, I didn't recognise you in your finery. You know me, don't you? Boy Mulcaster.'

'Yes duckie, ten bob each.'

We [Sebastian Flyte and Charles Ryder] paid, and the man who had been standing between us and the inner door now made way for us. Inside it was hot and crowded, for the Old Hundredth was at the height of its success. We found a table and ordered a bottle; the waiter took payment before he opened it.(10)

Mrs Meyrick was the widow of an Irish doctor from Brighton with eight children, six of them girls. She opened her first night-club supposedly to pay for their education. After a shaky start, she was fined £25, 'to deter her from further adventures in a sphere unsuited to the widows of doctors', and her licence was removed. From that club in Leicester Square, described by the magistrate as 'a sink of iniquity', she went on to open the most famous of all her clubs, 'The 43' at 43 Gerrard Street, in 1921. Like Ma Mayfield,

> Mrs Meyrick sat in a little office just inside the door, smiling her smile of welcome. She was a smallish woman, untidily dressed, with a sharp face and sharp eyes, and to all her visitors would say: 'Will you pay me now?'
>
> She was completely without glamour. Her clothes were dowdy. Against the wealthy, fabulously dressed visitors, she looked horribly out of place.
>
> Yet no other night-club owner achieved a tenth of her fame – not even the famous American, Texas Guinan. She was known to the whole world. Her exploits made luscious Sunday reading for millions.
>
> She was Kate Meyrick, the woman who made the '43' Club the greatest night-club in British history; whose peculiar business sense contrasted sharply with her open-handed generosity.(11)

'The 43', where Dryden once lived, was followed by a succession of other clubs, all of them popular, all of them fashionable. The 'Silver Slipper' in Regent Street was perhaps the smartest, where 'the walls were painted with Italian scenes, the dance floor [was] made of glass'.(12) Despite frequent raids by the police, the fines and her spells in prison (she was once in Holloway with a 'Colonel' Barker, a female embezzler dressed as a man) and the determination of the Home Secretary, William Joynson-Hicks, to stamp out what he termed 'licentiousness', she carried on manfully. Her list of clients was vast and varied, ranging from foreign royalty – King Carol of Rumania, Prince Nicholas of Rumania and the Crown Prince of Sweden – to the free-spending owners of Lancashire cotton-mills, although Mrs Meyrick found that 'the privilege of entertaining members of the peerage was a sentimental satisfaction; dukes seldom spent more than three pounds a night.'(13) This, however, did not prejudice her against the aristocracy, for three of her daughters married into the peerage; May married Lord Kinnoull, Dorothy married Lord de Clifford, and Gwendoline, the Earl of Craven.

The more respectable night-clubs, like 'Chez Victor's', the 'Kit-Kat' and the Embassy, with a more salubrious clientele, were equally liable to police raids. The Prince of Wales missed one raid on the Kit-Kat by just twenty-four hours. To be in a night-club during a raid was considered chic and something to be proud of. *Punch* showed a young girl being apprehended by a policeman and telephoning from a night-club: 'I shan't be home tonight Mummy, but its quite all right – we've been raided'.(14)

Victor, the owner of Chez Victor, was eventually closed down. His club in Grafton Street was different, being 'in a green Georgian room free from the usual night-club subterfuge of dimmed lights. Under the unfertive radiance of chandeliers, celebrated faces clustered round Indira Cooch Behar and Tallulah Bankhead who held court there nightly.'(15)

The most famous place of all was the Embassy Club. It was exclusive, with a drawing-room atmosphere about it: 'like going to a lovely party where one knew everyone'.(16) The Prince of Wales dubbed it 'that Buckingham Palace of night-clubs', and went there whenever he had a free night in London, often accompanied by Prince George.

The Embassy Club was at the end of a long and draughty passage ('pleurisy alley') between two shops at the lower end of Bond Street. Inside, swing doors opened on the long side of a well-proportioned room. The walls above the sofas and the tables were one huge mirror, reflecting the habitués, women such as Lady Cunard, Lady Louis Mountbatten and Mrs Richard Norton.

It was Mrs Richard Norton's table that Michael Arlen described in his novel, *The Green Hat*:

Nearby was a corner table of eight young people. Maybe they would dance later on. Suddenly, one of the girls would give a loud laugh and then there would be silence. Of the four young men one [the Hon. Richard Norton] looked as Richard of Gloucester might possibly have looked, a little bent, a little sinister, and pale, as though he had been reading a treatise on diseases far into the night before. They were four married couples, and they had been boys and girls together, and they had a son and a daughter apiece, and they all went to the same dentist. The one [Mrs Richard Norton] had a small oval face, small breasts, blue eyes, thin arms, no expression, no blood: literally, of course, not genea-logically. One of them stared with wide blue eyes right into people's faces, and blinked vaguely. She was lovely. These eight young people were very happy. They ignored every-thing but themselves, in whom they were not very inter-ested. Presently, a Prince of the blood [the Prince of Wales] joined them, there was a little stir for a minute or two, a little laughter, and then he rose to dance with the girl of the bright blue eyes. As she danced she stared thoughtfully at the glass dome of the ceiling. She looked bored with boredom.(17)

Whatever the venue, a sleezy or a smart night-club, restaurant or party, the young and the not so young danced at every given moment. As *Punch* commented: 'Smart society is said to be giving up breakfast. All doctors agree it is not wise to consume a heavy meal before going to bed.'

America was also responsible for two more imports – the cocktail and drugs. The former was to last, the latter, except for a few sad addicts, was just a passing craze. The chief ingredients of most cocktails are gin and vermouth. Gin was still considered a very low-class drink (shades of Dickensian penny drunk, two pence dead drunk); and vermouth, like absinth, had dangerous Parisian overtones. It was not long, however, before

the cocktail shaker became almost a symbol of the age . . . The original cocktails were three in number: the Martini (a mixture of gin and dry vermouth), the Manhattan (a mixture of Bourbon whiskey and sweet vermouth), and the Bronx (a mixture of gin, vermouth and fresh orange juice). But the bartenders, who became quite important personages, made it a point of honour to invent new varieties, some of which had strangely provocative names like 'Bosom Caresser', 'Maiden's Blush', 'Widow's Kiss' or 'Between the Sheets' . . . Some, like 'Some Moth', enshrined forgotten jokes; others, like 'Strikes Off', reflected the social upheavals of the twenties.(18)

11

THE GENERAL STRIKE

'We Seem to be Stuck in this Tunnel'

*I*N THE NINETEENTH CENTURY, there were only a few sources of employment considered fit for the younger sons of the wealthier upper classes and none at all for their daughters, whatever their origins and the source of their wealth. Traditionally, these younger sons entered the Church, the Services or the Bar, a few going abroad in administrative posts or with the Foreign Office. The war changed everything. The City no longer held the same stigma as in nineteenth-century Society; it was no longer vulgar to make money, even in trade. 'Fathers became insistent that their sons went out and found some gainful employment. It was thought very off if a man didn't have a job. Besides, fathers gave their sons pitiful allowances, so they had to work to make ends meet.'(1)

With the very real need to earn a living or to restore the family fortune, no job was too menial as long as it made money. Stockbroking and insurance firms initially regarded the invasion by these young men with scepticism: 'We want him for clerking, not for breeding purposes'.(2) Their connections often proved invaluable, however, and they were soon absorbed into the business world. Even fringe members of the Royal

Family, like the Marquesses of Carisbrooke and Cambridge, entered the City without comment.

The gossip columnists (also a new job for the aristocracy, headed by the Lords Castlerosse, Donegall and Kinross) regaled their readers with details of the unusual employment of Society: Cedric Alexander started a 'Social Bureau', shepherding Americans and other 'socially ambitious' people around Mayfair; Lord Bective became known as 'The Electric Earl' through founding an electrical company; Sir Joseph Tichborne became a bookmaker. The list was endless: the Hon. Anthony Vivian managed a theatre, Sir Harry Verney's heir sold loose-leaf ledgers, while Lord Trenchard recruited as many public schoolboys into the police force as possible. When Lord Settrington, the present Duke of Richmond and Gordon, came down from Oxford, he joined Bentley as an apprentice. When he was 'exposed' in an article in the *Chronicle*, his 'mates' called him over and announced: 'We likes you Fred, but you've got to lose that there Hoxford Haccent!'(3) Later, he went on to build his own cars and sell them through a showroom in Berkeley Square. Anthony Asquith's mother, Lady Oxford, said that he could only go into the film business 'over her dead body': she was to become his greatest fan.

Where once the aristocracy had been the driving force in politics, in the twenties they became the new force in the retail trade. It was a common complaint that it was impossible to go to a party without somebody trying to sell something. Instead of condemning these 'blacklegs of Mayfair', the traders exploited them, paying commission on introductions. Many women joined their ranks too, mostly with dress and hat shops, while Mrs Audrey Coates opened a scent shop in 1924 in Davis Street called 'Audrey's', and the Hon. Colonel and Mrs Fred Cripps had a hairdressing salon in Bond Street. Interior decorating businesses flourished; there were many 'Mrs Beavers' around, the foremost being Mrs Munro and, later, Mrs Somerset Maugham, Lady Colefax and John Fowler.

While men were expected to have a job of some sort, it was generally more difficult for women to work. However emancipated they became, upper-class women were still tied to the home, often through shortage of money. As a girl was seldom given much encouragement by her parents to do anything, only those of an independent spirit made the move and 'fled the nest'.

For many young women, good works, both in the country and London, occupied a small part of the day. Daphne Vivian started a crèche in East Ham. With two friends, she staggered there by bus twice a week to care for small babies. Others helped out in various clubs in the East End, but the visits mostly ended up as 'nothing so much as society hostesses without their tiaras'.(4) Many society women did do a great deal of selfless work in stricken areas. In 1923 there were 1,300,000 unemployed; there was widespread hunger and desperate hardship. Lady Airlie and her sisters, Lady Hambleden and Lady Salisbury, were typical when they volunteered to help the Reverend Ralph Eves in his parish of All Souls, Clapton Park, in the East End. They visited the parish, two afternoons a week, minding children while their mothers shopped, preparing meals for the old and infirm, and generally offering help and sympathy.

A private income of sorts was necessary to support a girl in London on her own, 'otherwise it was not worth working. A shopgirl at the General Trading [a smart gift shop by Sloane Square] earned £2 a week, which would not cover her board and lodging.'(5) But women did work, often as a means of escaping from home. Many took quite menial jobs, Lord Lonsdale's niece, Barbara Innes, even selling cars when hunting was stopped by foot-and-mouth disease in November 1924. Others found more interesting and responsible jobs in advertising and journalism – Lady Eleanor Smith and Lady Mary Clive both worked on London newspapers. The stage also became acceptable to women: the Ruthven identical twins, Alison and Margaret, called themselves the 'Ralli Twins' and danced in the music halls. Lady Diana Cooper began her stage and film career in 1922 with *The Great Adventurer*. In the past, many a girl started life as a mannequin or model and ended up as a 'Society beauty'; in the twenties, many a Society beauty did rather well as a model.

With the necessity of earning a living – and to most men in Society that meant working in London – came the problem of finding somewhere to live. Unless they could live at home, with all its incumbent restrictions, unmarried men either lived in lodgings (Ebury Street was nearly all smart lodging houses) or shared a flat with friends. As men spent every evening out, at restaurants, dinner parties or dances, occasionally at their clubs, it did not really matter where they stayed. The richer, obviously, had their own London establishments with a staff commensurate with their income.

With the demise of the great London houses came the new vogue for flats. Family houses were torn down and replaced with blocks of service flats, identical in every detail. Devonshire House was the first to be pulled down. In many of the more fashionable squares, like Portman Square, the large houses were converted into apartments. But flats did not suit everybody.

Those who could not afford a London house, in Mayfair or its environs, either moved into converted mews houses or 'migrated to the slums, where houses were small, with the result that mean streets around Westminster and Knightsbridge became fashionable'.(6)

The profligate living and Devil-may-care attitudes of the majority of the young society on the one hand, and the blinkered life of the old order on the other, amazingly co-existed against a background of economic depression and desperate hardship. It was not only the 1.3 million unemployed, eking out an existence on fifteen shillings a week, who were living in misery, but also those who were in work, many of whom were only marginally better off. The miners had struck in 1921 for a minimum wage, and won. In the spring of 1926, they threatened to strike again against the proposal to cut their wages and extend their working hours. The cry of 'Not a penny off the pay, not a minute on the day' was answered by the Trades Union Congress, who threatened to withdraw the labour of the key unions. A series of bungling decisions by Mr Baldwin's Government, coupled with the intransigence of the colliery owners, brought deadlock. When the TUC called the General Strike on Thursday, 4 May 1926, workers throughout Britain rallied to the call and set about bringing the country to a standstill. What the TUC leaders had not bargained for was the power of the middle and upper classes, and their determination to prevent any alteration to their life.

The call for volunteer labour went out shortly before the strike was actually declared. The response to help break the strike was immediate, men and women flooded into London – even Charles Ryder in *Brideshead* returned from Paris, one of 'the Black Birds newly arrived in England',(7) to join up. In all, three hundred thousand men and women, of all ages and all classes, especially the unemployed, seeing the promise of a job, signed on in the Voluntary Service Corps. From the very beginning, the strike-breaking machinery of the Government proved highly effective. In the days before the strike, Hyde Park was transformed into a vast centre for the distribution of milk and food; marquees were erected as canteens and rest centres for volunteer workers, manned mostly by débutantes and older Society women.

The more 'genteel' of the volunteers, recalled Lady Airlie, could repair to

the house in Grosvenor Place [where] dinner was kept going until after midnight for relays of girls helping on night shifts at the canteens that had been set up in Hyde Park to feed the volunteer lorry drivers. The firm that was responsible for the catering had fixed a charge of one shilling [5p.] a head for a meal of bacon, two eggs, two sausages, a slice of bread and butter and a cup of tea or coffee, which all the helpers complained was too expensive: which indeed it was by 1926 standards.

I spent a morning in one canteen working with a team of voluntary helpers headed by Molly Dalkeith [the present Dowager Duchess of Buccleuch] . . . The teams of amateur waitresses were all what were called 'society girls', looking exactly like ordinary working girls; no prettier, in fact looking rather more untidy. They were very tired – many of them were on duty fourteen hours a day behind the enormous tea-urns – but they were determined to carry on. The whole country had one resolve, to break the 'tyranny' of the strike.(8)

By the second day of the strike, a few trains, buses and trams were running, and two days later, nearly three thousand trains were run all over the country, all manned entirely by volunteers. For some, that childhood dream of becoming an engine driver was fulfilled, with the added attraction that the experience would not last long enough to become monotonous. It was no hardship for an Oxbridge undergraduate to drive a bus or a lorry; fortunately for them, the exigencies of the hour did not call for volunteers to go down a coal mine.

Such amateurism was all considered great fun: according to Beverley Nichols, exchanges like this were commonplace:
'We seem to be stuck in this tunnel, old boy.'
'What's the matter?'
'All the water seems to have come out of the old engine.'
'Can't we put some more in?'
'To tell the truth, old boy, I'm not quite sure how one puts the water in engines. Even when one's got the water to put in, which at the moment, one hasn't.'
'I suppose I'd better go and see if I can get another engine?'
'I say, old boy. That's jolly decent of you. There must be a spare knocking around somewhere in Liverpool Street.'
'I'll go right away.'
'Good idea. And by the way, I think it a good idea to put on the fog signals as you go down the line. We don't want a great walloping express crashing in our rear.'
'Where are the fog signals?'
'Don't you remember? They're those things by the side of

the rails that look like a sort of perverted poached eggs. They go off with a bang. Can't miss 'em.'

The young man wanders off into the Cimmerian darkness of the tunnel, in the direction of Liverpool Street, which is about two miles away. On the arm of his sports jacket he wears a band marked 'Guard No 4156'. As he walks, he reflects that this is a much pleasanter way of spending an evening than writing an essay on the Elizabethan ecclesiastical settlement for his tutor at Balliol. He rather hopes that the general strike will go on for quite a while. And then – he is not quite so sure. For as he emerges from the tunnel he is greeted by a hail of stones from a group of toughs on the bank above and shouts of 'Go back home, you bloody blackleg . . . go back home!' The young man decides that it might be politic to break into a sharp trot.

Incredible as it may sound, the young man got his engine from Liverpool Street Station . . . When they reached their destination, which was Stratford, they were only two hours late, and the passengers made a silver collection in a bucket, which was very acceptable to the young volunteers.

At the end of the general strike a grateful government gave Guard 4156 the sum of £4 5s 6d with which he rushed off to buy a Briggs umbrella, an object he had always coveted.

And then he went off to finish his essay on Elizabethan Settlement.(9)

The Oxford undergraduate was in illustrious company: 'Mr C. E. Pitman, the Oxford stroke, drove a train on the GWR from Bristol to Gloucester.'(10) Lord Chesham and the Hon. Lionel Guest were also train drivers. Lord Weymouth drove a lorry, 'unromantically driving ice to all the grand hotels'.(11) 'The Honourable Mrs Beaumont, with several other Society women, undertook stable duty at Paddington Station [most railway vans were horse drawn]. Lord Monkswell was a signalman.'(12)

Competition to drive more humble transport, such as a bus or a tram, was equally keen, as H. W. Austin found:

During my first summer term at Cambridge the normal lawn tennis programme was upset by the General Strike. However, the greater part of the University rejoiced at the prospect of being able to defeat the strikers. I went with a group of undergraduates to help conduct buses from their depot at Chiswick Park. Unfortunately, there were six hundred of us all equally keen to conduct the same bus.

After one or two idle days and uncomfortable nights endeavouring to sleep on top of the bus, and having contracted colds of considerable violence, a friend and myself took seats as passengers in one of the many buses we endeavoured to conduct. We went to look for work elsewhere and obtained an excellent job on the railway; but this was too much for the strikers, and before we were able to undertake our duties, the strike was at an end. After one or two pleasant days of golf, we returned to Cambridge to continue the term.(13)

The new bus drivers took no special route, and anyone who complained that they ended up miles from their destination was considered a 'spoil-sport'. One conductor directed his bus round Eaton Square to pick up his morning's post.

Despite the vagaries of the buses, offices continued to function. 'Thousands of strap-hangers went to their offices in the luxury of limousines. Tweed-clad women in two-seaters patrolled the roads of Kensington and Bayswater, and in some parts of London the chief difficulty was to enjoy a stroll, so importunate were the offers of "lifts".'(14)

Thousands joined up as special constables. The *Illustrated London News* went so far as to write, 'We feel that the heart of England must be sound when we read that the Headmaster of Eton [Dr Alington] and about fifty of his assistant masters have enrolled as special constables.'(15) Lord Grantley (then the Hon. Richard Norton) turned up at 'Whites, and a lot of us departed to join the Special Constabulary. We were given truncheons, whistles and uniforms; and after further adjustments to the latter by our tailors we were ready for duty.'(16) One of the group was 'Fruity' Metcalfe, the Prince of Wales's friend and Equerry. Four of them were told to report to Bethnal Green.

It struck me as asking for trouble, not to mention being the height of bad taste, to send round four rich young men in an expensive car, dressed up like idiots, their chests blazing with medal ribands ... Nothing happened. Not a baby shook a rattle at us. In fact the only incident was when some fellow broke a window . . .(17)

Charles Ryder, who joined 'Bill Meadows' show' formed from the members of Bratts, escorted a convoy of milk vans three times a day and spent the rest of the time at his new club. They were jeered at and 'sometimes pelted with muck'.(18) Once, to the delight of the rest of 'Bill Meadows' show', they went into action against a group of dockers. Although most of the country

*Cars queueing in the Mall – engines purring, debutantes' hearts a-flutter –
before a Royal Court.*

Beverley Nichols, clear-eyed chronicler of Society in the 1920s.

Right: conversation piece at a ball at Cowdray Park.

'Where on earth did you get that!' Princess Alice, Countess of Athlone, and Lady Alexander at a garden party at St James's Palace.

Cecil Beaton and his sister Nancy putting in an appearance at Lord's.

At Ascot the racing was magnificent, the dressage better still. The Royal Meeting was a Mecca of women's fashions.

Below: *hoisting the mainsail on the Royal Yacht* Britannia. *The King lends a hand.*

Bottom left: Britannia *leading* Velsheda, Candida, Shamrock, *and* Astra *to the starting line at Cowes.*

Right: *the first post-war Derby brought record-breaking crowds in spite of the rain and mud – 'almost as bad as in the trenches' – which dogged the event throughout the decade.*

Bottom right: *polo at Ranelagh in 1921. The club side tussles here with the strong American team which dented England's polo pride in a series of International matches at Hurlingham.*

Above: *on the tee at Gleneagles. It looks as if he may have to get her another ball.*

Left: *an exhibition of lawn tennis at West Hill, Highgate. By the 1920s every country house of note boasted a tennis court.*

'In those days the hunting was pure magic.' The stirrup cup is served at a lawn meet.

A shooting party on the Earl of Ancaster's moor at Drummond Castle.

A notable racing driver of the twenties, the Earl Howe, as seen by F. Gordon-Crosby.

A great day for MG at Brooklands, with MG Midgets taking the first four places in the twelve-hour race. Congratulations from MG's Managing Director for the winners, the Earl of March (the present Duke of Richmond and Gordon) and C. S. Staniland.

Above left: *the Duchess of
Bedford with her co-pilot
Captain Barnard at Croydon
Airport after flying to India
and back in a week. 'The
Flying Duchess' was one of
the most adventurous spirits
of the age, and was killed on
a solo flight at the age of
seventy-one.*

*The fishing in the 1920s was
exceptional. The Hon. Mrs
Macdonald and gillie at
Marrock Moor.*

*Lady Diana Cooper, the
Society beauty of the
twenties, with her husband
Duff at Deauville.*

The original Bright Young People pulled off some highly amusing and clever hoaxes. The discovery and launch of the German artist Bruno Hat was one of the best. **Right:** Hat's 'Adoration of the Magi', painted by Brian Howard. **Left:** The artist, impersonated by Tom Mitford.

The Mozart Party at the Burlington Galleries having come to an end, a group of Bright Young People try their hand at roadworks.

At the canteen run by Mrs Loeffler at
Scotland Yard, volunteers served meals to
the special constables, who included Dr
Alington, Headmaster, and fifty other Eton
masters.

The General Strike posed new problems,
but was generally welcomed by the young.
It broke down barriers (left) and provided
opportunities for a return to chivalry which
few could refuse.

was quiet, there were violent scenes – bus drivers stoned, cars overturned and burned, baton charges by the police and 'specials'.

On the evening of the first day of the strike, the *Morning Post* invited the Government to commandeer their presses and offices to produce an official bulletin. Under the general direction of Winston Churchill, the *British Gazette* was founded. It voiced the views of the Government, Winston Churchill telling the public just as much as he thought they ought to know, which was not much. Nearly a quarter of a million copies of the single-sided *British Gazette* came out every day of the strike, the presses all manned by volunteers. Lord Hambleden's nephews, Robin and Arthur Ackland, 'sat up night after night at the works printing the *British Gazette* . . . Billy Smith went round with a van delivering them.'[19]

The *Times* also produced a single sheet. In its own words, it became 'the very centre of fashion'. Among its lorry drivers were the Duchess of Sutherland, the Duchess of Westminster, Viscountess Massereene and Ferrard and Lady Maureen Stanley. Throughout the strike, *The Times* building was picketed but the strikers all touched their caps when the proprietor, Major Astor, walked through their lines. Among the emergency work force on the presses were Graham Greene, domestic staff from Major Astor's town house, a chauffeur and eight gardeners from Hever Castle, his place in Kent. The *Daily Mail* was printed in Paris and flown over. Although a single sheet, it still managed to inform its readers of the divorce of a peer, who subsequently went to gaol, and the marginal effect of the strike on Society.

COVENT GARDEN PACKED

The Grand Opera season at Covent Garden opened on Monday night. The huge auditorium was packed from floor to ceiling, with very few empty seats.

The stalls and Boxes were filled with men in white ties, and tail coats, but although on the surface the house seemed as brilliant as usual, on a close examination it was apparent that the women's dresses had a subdued note and that the true elegance and sparkle of fashion was being reserved for the later and more auspicious occasion.[20]

There were a few exceptions to the middle- and upper-class strike-breakers. Those with a more developed social conscience, men like Hugh Gaitskell, who acted as the liaison between the TUC units in Oxford and London, ran the gauntlet of their fellow undergraduates and tutors. Although half his college were away 'answering the call', the Warden, the historian H. A. L. Fisher, fined him one pound for climbing in after midnight. Christoper Isherwood was torn between class loyalty and political sympathy. In the end, he did not have to decide, for the strike was over: 'The Poshocracy had won, as it always did win, in thoroughly gentlemanly manner . . . it was quite prepared magnanimously to pretend that nothing more serious had taken place than, so to speak, a jolly sham fight with pats of butter.'(21)

The strikers felt they had been let down and were worse off than before the strike. To the unemployed, the strike was over too quickly and, once again, they were without a job. To the majority of the strike-breakers, it was just a lark, great fun while it lasted. One girl who worked in the canteen thought it 'splendid as, unlike the First War, it did not go on long enough to get boring'.

12

THE BRIGHT YOUNG PEOPLE

'Young and Hungry, Wild and Free'

MUCH HAS BEEN WRITTEN ON the younger generation during the twenties, both at the time and in retrospect. Evelyn Waugh satirised them in his wickedly amusing novel, *Vile Bodies*, although those whom he parodied thought he had gone too far. Jacques Reval (the author Jack Laver) went even further in his *Woman of 1926* when he singled out the modern woman as depraved hedonist:

Mother's advice, and father's fears,
Alike are voted just a bore,
There's negro music in our ears,
The world is one huge dancing floor.
We mean to tread the Primrose Path,
In spite of Mr Joynson-Hicks.
We're people of the Aftermath,
We're girls of 1926.

In greedy haste, on pleasure bent,
We have no time to think, or feel,
What need is there for sentiment
Now we've invented Sex-Appeal?
We've silken legs and scarlet lips,

We're young and hungry, wild and free.
Our waists are round about our hips,
Our skirts are well above the knee.

We've boyish busts and Eton Crops,
We quiver to the saxophone,
Come dance before the music stops,
And who can bear to be alone?
Come, drink your gin, or sniff your 'snow',
Since Youth is brief and Love has wings,
And Time will tarnish, ere we know
The brightness of the Bright Young Things.(1)

The Bright Young People, as the originators were called ('things', although rhyming nicely with 'wings', is incorrect), became the generic term for any decadent members of the younger generation who behaved badly, or irresponsibly, during the latter half of the 1920s. Yet at the outset, the precursors of what the Press dubbed the 'Society of the Bright Young People' were just a few select friends who were amusing, with like, impulsive natures and a great capacity for enjoyment. Their exploits showed an outward personality, their attitude an impromptu demonstration against the dullness and conventionality of social life. Their antics were essentially harmless, often directed against people's social or intellectual pretensions. When their numbers grew and their escapades were copied without the originality or style of the founders, those founders dropped out and left the field to the exhibitionists whose parties 'always seemed to be held where there were photographers and where they would create the maximum disturbance.'(2)

The favourite amusements of the 'founding' Bright Young People were treasure hunts and hoaxes. Their practical jokes were carefully worked out and combined skilful acting and a great deal of nerve. The three prime movers were the Jungman sisters, Zita and Theresa (known as 'Baby', a name she disliked and eventually managed to discard), the daughters of Beatrice Guinness by her first marriage, and Lady Eleanor Smith, the daughter of Lord Birkenhead. Lady Lindsay remembers Eleanor as 'a strange, fiery, uninhibited creature with a handsome head that looked as if it had been chipped out of some hard material, violent in her likes and dislikes and a rebel against convention. She was also a torrential and amusing talker.'(3) A favourite practical joke was for 'Baby' Jungman, posing as Eleanor Smith's young stepmother, to interview the headmistresses of various girls' schools with a view to placing her there. The late Lord Birkenhead wrote of their most successful imposture, when they dressed

Baby, aged fifteen, as 'Mme Anna Vorolsky', a Russian refugee, with priceless jewels to sell, to pay, as she explained with long, downcast lashes, 'for the education of my poor little boy'.

The success of this impersonation was extraordinary. They dressed the child in a long black velvet dress and her mother's mink coat. She wore a black wig and a rope of Woolworth's pearls. Her face was made up a deadly white and her mouth a scarlet wound. She spoke with a foreign accent, in a husky, seductive contralto, and a disturbing aroma of Geurlain's 'Mitsouko' hung around her.(4)

Thus primed, they went in search of victims. She lunched with Beverley Nichols at a dimly lit restaurant, clutching an empty jewel case, and, with Eleanor and Zita hiding under the table, she poured out her troubles to the sympathetic author. She regaled the Duke of Marlborough with stories of the Red Terror in Russia.

'And so, I have lost everything' – a sob – 'except my dear little boy.'
'I had no idea, madame, that such terrible things had happened in your ravaged country,' said the Duke earnestly.'(5)

Flushed with success, she took the tease too far. At a garden party, she arrived with two borzois and a 'purple orchid glowing malignantly on her corsage'. Presented to an elderly general, she murmured,

'Oh Seer Enry – Navair shall I forget that *wonderful* night we spent together in Paris in the war.'
The General flushed and looked anxiously at his wife.
'To the best of my recollections, madame,' he replied coldly, 'I spent only one night in Paris in the whole war.'
'Zat', replied Baby archly, 'was zee night.'(6)

The innocent General's reputation in ruins, 'Madame Vorolski' left the country in a hurry. Her place was taken by a 'reporter', Miss Gooch, alias – at various times – Lady Eleanor Smith, Baby and Zita Jungman. Eleanor had a neat business card printed:

Miss Babington Gooch
Amalgamated Provincial Press

With this bogus, flimsy credential, they would go off to interview celebrities staying at the smarter London hotels. Their list of victims was impressive, although Lilian Gish saw through them immediately, as did John Barrymore.

Russian émigrés were also good for impersonation. Lord Kinross recounted how he had been staying in the country when some neighbours came in for tea bringing with them 'Prince Michael of Serbia'. He was, in fact, an MP and had been at Eton with one of the house party. Everyone treated him with due deference and addressed him as 'Sir', he entered and left the room first (being an Etonian, this, no doubt, came easily to him). After tea, the 'Prince' played bridge with Kinross and two girls, who were in such a twitter of excitement that they had difficulty in concentrating on their cards. The 'Prince', flaunting his royal prerogative, cheated shamelessly and openly revoked. Kinross, fearful of committing lese-majesty, ignored it, the girls were too confused to notice. Later he confided with one of them that he had narrowly escaped death travelling at 60 mph.

'I had no chauffeur', he explained, 'because sometimes a prince likes to escape from his subjects, you understand. I knew little of mechanics, but after a long struggle was able to put on a new wheel. When I got back to Belgrade I found that the wheel was hanging by a thread. It was a miracle that it had not flown off. For do you know what I had done? I had put the wheel on *upside down*!'

The girl was aghast. 'Oh, *sir*,' she said, 'what a terrible experience! And what sort of a car was it?'

'A Hispano-Suiza.'

'How lovely!' was her comment, 'I always think Rolls-Royces are so slow, don't you?'

The hoax only leaked out sometime later.(7)

The most ingenious of all the hoaxes of the time was the exhibition of the paintings of the German 'artist', Bruno Hat. It was conceived by Brian Howard and brilliantly executed with the help of his friends and Evelyn Waugh. He began by leaking the story to Lady Eleanor Smith (then a bona-fide journalist writing a column 'From my Window in Vanity Fair' in the *Sunday Dispatch*), who wrote:

BRUNO HAT. What will be almost a cocktail party, is a private view of the exhibition of paintings by Bruno Hat, to be held next week. Bruno Hat is a painter of German extraction, and his work is mainly of the abstract type, seemingly derivative of Picasso and Chirico. But the queer thing is that his work is not derived from any painter – he was discovered by Mr Bryan Guinness near Clymping. Bryan Guinness went into the village general store, and entering by mistake the wrong room, he found a number of very good paintings in the modern French style.

The paintings were done by the son of the old lady who keeps the store. His father was a German, and he paints quite naturally without ever having been to Paris. In fact, he had only been to London about twenty times in his life, being very shy and retiring. So good are the paintings, that they are to be on exhibition at Mr Bryan Guinness's house in Westminster. I have seen one or two, and they are surprisingly clever.(8)

There were twenty paintings in all, painted by Brian Howard in John Banting's studio. Some were painted on cork bath mats and framed, for reasons of economy, with white rope. Lady Mosley (then Mrs Bryan Guinness) recalled that 'Brian and Banting rushed up the stairs with several pictures under each arm, and their excitement when the whole lot were hung in the drawing room [in Buckingham Street] was contagious.(9)

The preface of the catalogue, *The Approach to Hat*, was written by Evelyn Waugh, a parody of the usual art jargon:

Mr Bruno Hat came to England with his father in 1919 from Lübeck. After having lived in this country for a short time, Mr Max Hat married an Englishwoman, and bought a general dealer's shop in Sussex, where he lived until he died in 1923. The shop is now managed by Mr Bruno Hat with the help of his stepmother.

Mr Bruno Hat is now thirty-one years of age. Apart from some two months or so at Hamburg Art School, he is entirely self taught. In frequent visits to London, exhibitions have provided him with little more than a glimpse of contemporary movements in painting. He has never, until now, exhibited a picture. A month ago, however, several examples of his work were taken to Paris, and the opinion there was so immediately favourable that successful arrangements have been made for an exhibition there in the early winter.

A. R. de T.(10)

To the annoyance of the real artist, Brian Howard, Tom Mitford, Lady Mosley's brother, was dressed up as the artist and on that night (23 July 1929) sat in a bath chair in the corner dressed in 'the sort of black clothes a penniless German artist might easily wear if he had put on his "Sunday best" for the occasion'.(11) He was disguised with a 'moustache worthy of Harry Tate and smoked glasses. In one hand he held a thin cheroot, in the other a glass of iced coffee, and as he sipped and puffed he grumbled about the colour of the walls and about the publicity he was receiving.'(12)

The evening was a splendid success and, as expected, both the intelligentsia of Mayfair and the art critics 'came in droves'.(13) Lady Mosley is convinced that everyone knew that it was a joke; Lytton Strachey went so far as actually to buy a picture to please her so that she could put up a red 'sold' spot. However, many, including the Press, were totally taken in by the hoax and wrote it up in their gossip columns. The Dragoman used such phrases as 'Mrs Converse . . . stood in apparent rapture before the exhibits' and 'some of the pretty girls who stood looking at Mr Hat or drinking Mrs Guinness's excellent cocktails seemed . . . a little overwhelmed.'(14) He invented an exchange between the young Oxford don, Maurice Bowra, and 'Mr Hat', in which the latter replied to a torrent of German, 'I am naturalised Englisch. I do not care to remember that I speak Cherman.' Tom Mitford, in fact, spoke better German than Bowra. It was a splendid joke that hurt no one except possibly the main perpetrator, Brian Howard, who, in some way, 'had hoped for a Hollywood-style miracle, and that he would be "discovered" by an astonished art world as a master'.(15)

The other twenties phenomenon, the treasure hunt, grew from an innocuous piece of fun devised by Eleanor Smith as an amusing diversion for a boring afternoon. What she and her friends, Baby and Zita Jungman and Enid Raphael, failed to realise was that they 'were unwittingly blazing a trail that led directly to a phenomenon she most detested: the Bright Young People.'(16)

Zita and Eleanor were the hares with five minutes' start, and they zig-zagged about London using buses and undergrounds and leaving clues behind as they went. This turned out to be such an exciting game that they asked me [Lady Lindsay] and some other girls to join in, and we used to amuse ourselves on blank afternoons by chasing each other round London.(17)

The game soon became more sophisticated, with a pre-planned route to places further apart. The clues were generally cryptic, some more obscure, like those written in international shipping flags or in morse code. At that level, it was great fun, harmless, and it was not long before more and more of their friends clamoured to join in. As the majority of the men were working, the longer treasure hunts started after dinner, so changing the character and nature of the game. Instead of quietly leaping on and off buses and undergrounds, they travelled by car.

The contestants met at some pre-arranged place, such as Horse Guards Parade, where they were given the first clue. From then on, they 'behaved like Furies'. With no traffic lights to hold them up, they roared all over London, shrieking and hooting horns as they pursued the next clue, regardless of those trying to sleep. The faster the car, the better; some hired cars if their own were not fast enough, others bribed taxi drivers to guide them around the back streets. Lady Diana Cooper was an adept treasure-hunter. One typical night took her

to the Achilles Statue ('A vulnerable point in Hyde Park'), a postcard of the Death of Chatterton then led her to the Tate Gallery where a messenger boy gave the next clue: 'Not far from here, the warriors of the Crimea have a garden.' From the Pensioners' Garden in Chelsea an anagram took her to the statue of Peter Pan in Kensington Gardens and thence ('Dury Lane. Look out for Nell Gwynne') to Viola Parsons dressed as an orange girl and onto the treasure in a letter box in Woburn Square. Diana completed the course in two hours ten minutes and came second.(18)

On one treasure hunt, a clue was hidden by Buckingham Palace, when the contestants 'bore down on the sleeping Palace with screeching tyres, jumped out of the cars and rushed up and down the railings, looking for the clue in the sentry boxes and shouting and screaming while every moment more cars kept arriving.'(19) The next day it was revealed that the Captain of the Guard had turned out all available men and called up for reinforcements, believing that the Palace was under seige. The clue was, in fact, at the foot of the memorial to Queen Victoria: a bunch of white roses with a card printed: 'All good Cavaliers will know where this should be laid'. They left, of course, for Charles I's statue in Trafalgar Square.

The clues became more and more elaborate, sometimes with help from surprising quarters. At their bread factory on the Embankment, Hovis gave everyone a small, brown loaf with the next clue baked inside. On another occasion, Lord Beaverbrook printed a special edition of *The Evening Standard* with the clue hidden inside the fake news. As the field increased, so the prize for the winner grew, often as much as £100 [£1,576 today]. The large prize sometimes led to chicanery, and anyone without all the clues was disqualified.

With such a large field, it was inevitable that the treasure hunts would be written up in the Press. The first account appeared in the *Daily Mail* in 1924:

NEW SOCIETY GAME
MIDNIGHT CHASE IN LONDON
50 MOTOR CARS
THE BRIGHT YOUNG PEOPLE

. . . By this time slow cars had given place to high-powered ones, and slow wits to faster wits, so that the field, which started at some fifty cars strong, all closely packed, jostling and manoeuvering for position, was straggled out, though still travelling well.

Lovely coiffures and beautiful dresses deftly arranged were no longer in that form. Shingled heads scored heavily, for long hair in many cases streaming in the breeze. Dressmakers should rejoice at the birth of the Bright Young People, for few of the frocks that went to Seven Dials yesterday morning will ever see the light of the ballroom again. A crawl on all fours in that none too clean neighbourhood . . . in search of an elusive clue walked on the pavement, had soiled the majority beyond repair.

The hunters found their final clue in Norfolk House, St James's, and here a splendid breakfast had been prepared and a string band to cheer them after their strenuous adventures.'(20)

For the Bright Young People, everything was done in the name of fun, adventure and, most of all, originality. After a dinner at Phyllis Court near Henley on Thames on the eve of Lord Faringdon's wedding, the guests poured eight two-gallon cans of petrol on to the river. Under the direction of Brian Howard, they 'set the Thames on fire'. Howard also led a 'conger' through the department store, Selfridges, 'a game', recalled the Marquess of Bath, 'which would not be tolerated in these days, but the management took it extraordinarily well. There must have been two dozen of us at least, jumping on the counters and doing everything which Brian did.'(21)

That group believed that they had *carte blanche* to behave exactly as they wished. Daphne Fielding wrote of their visit to the Fun Fair at Wembley, where there was a side show called 'The River Caves':

. . . little boats floated through dark, subterranean caverns past illuminated troglodyte scenes, including one of Dante's Inferno, where papier mâché figures, chained to cardboard rocks, writhed in paper flames and an enormous scarlet Mephistopholes poked his pitch fork into victims.

As the boats drifted past, we would jump out and land among the lost souls in Hades and play our ukeleles, while Brian Howard, looking like a sinister Spielmann, defied the Devil, who seemed insignificant beside him. Meanwhile our boats, one after the other, floated back empty; and we would have to take off our shoes and stockings and paddle to the entrance, where we made a barefoot getaway from the angry attendants.(22)

Such adventures soon lost their exclusiveness, and, 'every wild party, Bohemian rag or large scale practical joke which took place in the West End between 1924 and 1930 was supposed to have been perpetrated by these Bright Young People'.(23) The original group bowed out when they were taken over by those 'in Rolls-Royces and Bentleys screaming through the East End, watched with loathing by early risers of the neighbourhood.'(24)

Bizarre and outrageous parties were for the young, and the not so young, a constant source of amusement throughout the decade. Venue and originality were everything, which invariably included dressing-up and a theme. Adam Fenwick-Smyth, the protagonist of Evelyn Waugh's *Vile Bodies*, sighed:

'Oh, Nina, *what a lot of parties* . . . Masked parties, Savage parties, Victorian parties, Greek parties, Russian parties, Circus parties, parties where one had to dress as somebody else, almost naked parties in St John's Wood, parties in flats and studios and houses and hotels and night-clubs, in windmills and swimming-baths, tea parties at school where one ate muffins and meringues and tinned crab, parties at Oxford where one drank brown sherry and smoked Turkish cigarettes, dull dances in London and comic dances in Scotland and disgusting dances in Paris – all that succession and repetition of massed humanity . . . Those vile bodies . . .(25)

Evelyn Waugh must surely have only had to flick through his own diaries recording such 'freak' parties to paint such a picture. The most imaginative parties, however, sprang from the more artistic, such as David Tennant and Brian Howard. It was David and Hermione Tennant who gave the Mozart Party at the Burlington Galleries where all the guests wore eighteenth-century dress. A small string orchestra played the 'Jupiter Symphony' as the guests arrived, followed by a magnificent supper and dancing. A photograph appeared next day in the paper of the 'survivors' with some roadmen digging up the street.

It was also Brian Howard who devised an ambitious party in

the Greek (as opposed to the freak) style. The printed invitation, over sixteen inches high and nearly twelve inches wide, was headed THE GREAT URBAN DIONYSIA. On either side, in columns headed *J'accuse* and *J'adore*, were listed the host's pet hates and his present loves respectively. The centre was 'taken up by lengthy instruction of the honoured guests and extracts from Jean Desbordes' *J'adore* and Cocteau's preface to that work, and the paragraphs decoratively divided by typographical ornaments of a wine-bibbling nymph and a spreading vine pendulous with ripe bunches of grapes.'(26) Brian Howard went to immense trouble over the arrangements with endless research in the British Museum. The guests joined in the spirit of the party: the hostess, Mrs Plunket Greene, wore a 'beautiful blue dress copied from a vase and a wig fashioned in the Greek style of hairdressing';(27) Ernest Thesiger wore the menacing black robes of Medusa, while John Banting went as Mercury *à la Cocteau* with a winged engine driver's hat. Frank Pakenham (the present Lord Longford) went as Dionysus. '. . . with vine leaves in his hair, a leopard skin and little else, he encountered Beverley Nichols. Nichols surveyed him for a few seconds in pure horror. Then, "a mistake, I think," he shuddered and walked away.'(28)

Unfortunately, in spite of all Brian Howard's preparations, the party was not an outstanding success. For the climax, a bull was to transport Olivia Wyndham, dressed as Minerva, to her throne, but the bull never arrived. After that, the party fell rather flat as 'Domino' of the *Evening Standard* reported the next day:

> Last night a number of young Society people discovered the tedium of immortality . . . 'The Great Urban Dionysia' was what they called the party, but at moments it was definitely sub-urban in its lack of excitement . . . the party was so wonderfully well staged that one was almost persuaded to take one's immortality seriously, and that is fatal.
>
>   There were, in fact, some wonderful costumes; everybody had to be dressed as a character in Greek mythology.(29)

Norman Hartnell, just making his name as a dress designer, gave a 'Circus Party' in a peeress's house. (He had in fact taken it for the year of the sake of the one night of the party.) The invitation read, 'Come as a Circus Character', and the fact that only 250 guests were invited led to considerable competition for the invitation. '. . . performing wolves skipped merrily around the arena, there were acrobats, a performing seal and somewhat lethargic bear, and other stunts . . . Lady Eleanor Smith, who led a pony up the stairs, was continually asked if she was part of the show . . . There was a boat, which you sat in and promptly fell out of . . . Lady Diana Cooper's face was bright green.'(30)

Tremendous care went into producing the right and most original costume. For the Wild West Party, given by fifteen bachelors in Lancaster Gate, 'some of the smartest and prettiest women in London have been searching wildly for an appropriate dress . . . cowboy costumes are at a premium.'(31) Some went to the East End to have their clothes made up and, as Donald Rolf recalled, 'The great fun was getting ready for the occasion, making all the preparations, dressing up. The actual party was often a bit of an anticlimax.' The *Evening Standard* described the hosts: '"Hal" Acton was "Owner of the Premises", Lord Donegall, "General Bottle-Washer", and "Jumbo" Joliffe was "Chief Poisoner". *No matrimonial Hoofing* was the legend that confronted those who wanted to dance, and the rule did not need an intolerable effort on the part of such as obeyed it.'(32)

Such parties were not confined to the impecunious young. The Duchess of Sutherland gave an annual fancy dress ball at Hampden House in Green Street. Some of the dresses were magnificent, others were supposed to be amusing: one year, eight 'fashionable and elegant ladies went as the Eton College rowing eight. They brought their boat with them and, coxed by Mr Duff Cooper, rowed themselves into the ballroom.'(33) Lord Birkenhead went as Captain Hook and surprised everyone by bringing his twelve-year-old daughter, Pamela, dressed as Peter Pan; Lord Blandford elected to be a female Channel swimmer. The hostess changed several times during the evening. At another of her balls, Lord Portarlington and his son came as a hideous Victorian dowager and 'her' beautiful daughter, while Lord Berners came as a white monkey bride.

There was also a great vogue for impersonation parties, 'Come as somebody else', 'Come as your dearest enemy', 'Come as your opposite' or 'Come as your secret self'. Captain Neil McEachern started the craze by asking everyone to dress as another of the guests at the party. Tom Driberg went as Brian Howard, his face made up with one eyebrow given 'much more of an exaggerated twist. One of Brian's was always raised in that mocking satirical twist.'(34) Sir Martin Wilson went as 'Queen Mary in yachting costume – about 1910 period – white moire silk, stiff skirt, and an enormous powdered wig and toque to top it all.'(35) Oliver Messel went as Tallulah Bankhead in 'her garden of Eden dress', and with a mask of her face – his speciality.

Allanah Harper, a schoolfriend of the Jungman sisters, and

very much part of the scene, recalled those parties with mixed feelings:

So much has been written about the parties in the twenties. I must admit that I enjoyed them at the time, but on looking back upon them now, they appear like a Jerome Boche [sic] hell. There were so many parties, but two remain particularly in my mind, one because I was one of the hosts and the other because it took place in a swimming bath.

The first was called the Sailor party, everyone had to be dressed as a French sailor. I think the only exception was Raymond Mortimer, who came as a 'sponge bag', and Mrs Christabel McLaren, who was regal as 'Rule Britannia'. Tallulah Bankhead, dressed in wide English sailor's trousers, was the noisiest person in the room, and her cacophonous laughter made it difficult to hear the band. Lytton Strachey came resplendent as an Admiral, but being both an amateur Admiral and dancer he got his sword between his legs and fell down, from which disadvantageous position he was rescued by Brian [Howard] and Clive Bell. Soon afterwards I left, but heard that poor Gerald Reitlinger (who kindly lent his house for the party) had to throw embracing couples – still clinging to each other – out into the street at five in the morning.(36)

The swimming party Allanah Harper referred to was another of Brian Howard's ideas, a party co-hosted with Mrs Plunket Greene, Edward Gaythorne Hardy and Elizabeth Ponsonby (thought to be the model for Nina Blount in *Vile Bodies*). A printed card invited the guests to the

St George's Swimming Baths
Buckingham Palace Road
at 11 p.m. on Friday, 13th July, 1928.
Please wear a Bathing Suit
and bring a
Bath Towel and a Bottle

Tom Driberg, the Dragoman in the *Daily Express*, was the only gossip columnist to write first-hand copy. Throughout the evening, he ran to the nearest telephone box to keep his paper abreast of the events. The next morning's edition carried the full story:

Bathing costumes of the most dazzling kinds were worn by the guests. Dancing took place to the strains of a negro orchestra, and the hardy leaped later into the bath, of which the water had been slightly warmed.

Great rubber horses and flowers floated about the water, which was illuminated by coloured spotlights. Many of those present brought two or three bathing costumes, which they changed in the course of the night's festivities. Cocktails were served in the gallery, where the cocktail mixers evidently found the heat intolerable for they also donned bathing costumes at the earliest possible opportunity. A special cocktail, christened the Bathwater Cocktail, was invented for the occasion.

The Hon. Stephen Tennant . . . wore a pink vest and long blue trousers. Mr Clive Bell was another there, and Miss Elizabeth Ponsonby looked most attractive in a silk bathing costume of which the lower part was red and the bodice rainbow-like with its stripes of blue and red.(37)

The party lasted all night and the bedraggled guests left to the censorious glares of the workers in the early hours of the morning. The police were called to clear the remaining guests from the pool and it appeared that 'their efforts were somewhat hampered by the more rapacious ones dragging them off to the changing-room cubicles – in the hope of general disrobing.'(38) Although the party was held at the height of a heatwave and the idea seemed reasonable enough, public opinon was outraged at their behaviour. The *Sunday Chronicle* reported:

Great astonishment and not a little indignation is being expressed in London over the revelation that in the early hours of yesterday morning a large number of Society women danced in bathing dresses to the music of a negro band at a 'swim and dance' gathering organised by some of Mayfair's Bright Young People.(39)

'A well-known Society hostess' (probably the reporter) objected to the negro band. 'It seems to me wholly wrong to introduce a coloured element to a scene where white men and women, though they may be thoroughly enjoying themselves, are not appearing in the most dignified role.'(40) To the Bright Young People, who courted publicity, such comments made the party all the more worthwhile.

'Bottle parties' had long been a feature of the Bright Young People, who made the most of their often meagre resources. The claim of Loelia Ponsonby (the present Lady Lindsay) that she was the founder of the 'bottle party' has been corroborated by Cecil Beaton:

In London during the twenties, Miss Ponsonby was one of

the instigators of a new type of gala. She lived with her parents in St James's Palace (where her father held a position close to the King), and preferred less conventional parties to those attended by other courtiers and their folk. Miss Ponsonby would, on an impulse, arrange a last-minute party and ask her friends to contribute an essential ingredient: some benevolent godfather would supply a band, other guests provided supper, all brought champagne. Nancy Mitford, and a bevy of new personalities just down from Oxford, Lord Kinross, Evelyn Waugh, Harold Acton and Oliver Messel [he was never up at Oxford], who were either of the aristocracy or entertained the aristocracy by their talents.(41)

Lady Lindsay wrote of a party she gave in November 1926:

Quite by chance . . . my brother and I were alone in our house in St James's, our parents being away on the inevitable round of shooting visits. There was the large drawing-room and parquet floor but, as usual, we were short of money, so we asked the girls to bring the food and the men the drink. It worked out perfectly. On arrival, each guest was relieved of a discreet parcel which was unpacked and laid out in the dining-room and the success of the evening was assured when Michael Arlen, gallant as always, arrived with a dozen bottles of pink champagne. The music was provided, rather unevenly, by the guests, who strummed on the piano, and Oliver Messel gave a one-man cabaret show. In retrospect, his imitations appear in dubious taste, but at the time we thought them excruciatingly funny. My parents, on their return, took it all very calmly, but the Press got hold of the story and wrote it up luridly as 'The Bottle Party' and our impromptu gathering of friends became the ancestor of many a squalid, law-evading orgy.(42)

To the older generation, bottle was a word that suggested squalor; a bottle party evoked in their minds a picture of 'sprawling individuals drinking neat gin out of bottles; and when David Tennant gave a "pyjama and bottle party" the picture of abandonment was complete.'(43) The party provided the newspapers with unlimited copy, the *Daily News* version being:

The hundreds of guests came in pyjamas the colours of which might be the envy of the foremost futurist artist of the day. The first arrival was a pretty flaxen-haired girl of about nineteen, wearing pyjamas with stripes of salmon pink, blue, red, green, orange and white. Her contribution was a bottle of 1840 champagne which was immediately consumed. Mr and Mrs David Tennant (the host and hostess) were attired in sleeping suits of orange. Many of the men's pyjamas were trimmed with lace. The bottles of refreshments which the guests were expected to bring provided an amusing diversion. The second bottle was gin; the third, hair-restorer; the fourth, health-salts; and other bottles included distilled water, beer, ink, petrol, Ethyl, smelling salts, Thames water, Jordan water, cabbage water, and water from a pool alive with tadpoles. The party was supposed to drink these 'refreshments' . . . All the while, in another room, the orchestra was playing dreamy music.(44)

The one party that enraged the public more than any other was the 'Baby Party', the invitation to which read:

> *We are having a Party with Romps*
> *from ten o'clock to bedtime.*
> *Do write and say you'll come,*
> *and we'd love to have Nanny too,*
> *Pram Park provided.*
> *Dress:*
> *Anything from birth to school age.*

The invitation to return to the cradle proved irresistible, and for the hosts and guests it was a 'howling success'. The *Daily Express* carried the story in full:

The so-called young people arrived in perambulators. They rode rocking horses in the gardens, chased each other on donkeys and scooters, and bowled hoops. Screams resounded in the brightly lighted square (Rutland Gate, Knightsbridge). The guests were dressed as babies in long clothes, Boy Scouts, Girl Guides, and nurses. They chased each other round the square with comforters in their mouths, carrying toy boats, dolls, and pails and spades. An attempt was made to take the donkeys into the house. They were led up the steps, the butler pushing from behind. Three sailor boys were mounted on the animals, but the floor of the hall was too slippery for them, and they fell to the ground, scattering their riders among the screaming 'children', who crowded the stairway. While some of the guests played in the garden, others amused themselves in the house by playing with trains and other mechanical toys. Late in the evening, the crowd was scattered by the violent ringing of a fire-bell. It was only some of the Bright Young People arriving in a taxi-cab. Cocktails were served in nursery mugs, and the bar was a babies' pen.(45)

For the guests, the party was made more memorable by the complaints of the neighbours, who were kept awake until four o'clock, and the large crowd of onlookers that gathered in the square. The latter shouted their disapproval over the railings, some going as far as to sing 'The Red Flag'. Newspapers were full of condemnation of the party, one even describing it as 'an outrage on the public, and an insult to the innocence of childhood'. F. R. Holmes voiced his disapproval in verse:

Bring your toys and Teddies.
Come prepared to crawl,
Shake a wicked rattle at the pop-eyed Babies' Ball,
Choose your socks and rompers,
Sport a sailor suit,
Bonnets trimmed with pompoms look most infantile and
    'cute'.
Armed with bibs and bottles,
Prattle and say 'Ga!',
Suck a naughty cocktail at the Bad Boys' Nursery Bar,
Bright Young Things of thirty,
Seeking Life and Colour,
Won't 'oo 'tum and toddle, long time past bedtime wiz
    Abdulla?(46)

This baby theme continued: at the Duchess of Sutherland's ball, even the Prince of Wales and the Duke of Kent came dressed as little boys with velvet suits, while Lord Ednam and Fred Cripps dressed as nannies and wheeled Lady Ednam and the Duchess of Westminster in prams, both wearing nappies and hideous baby-masks.

By the end of the decade, the Bright Young People had burned and played themselves out. (In *Vile Bodies* there are two violent deaths and a suicide.) Their parties were written up in the police and coroners' courts rather than the gossip columns. At one party in Chelsea, a man fell to his death from the second floor window. When the doctor arrived to tend him, a guest threatened him with a knife. At another party, a man had his eyes gouged out; at a third, a girl had her ear-drum broken. Allanah Harper remembers that the last 'theme party' she went to ended in a free fight and she found herself 'in the middle of a jealous fracas, scuffle and scrimmage, which although it had nothing to do with me, resulted in my dress being practically torn off and tufts of my hair held up as trophies. After that experience, I never went to parties of that sort ever again.'(47)

The swansong of the Bright Young People finally came in 1931 when Sandy Baird gave an 'All White Party' at his mother's house in Kent. John Banting decorated the barn with various objects, including a bicycle and garden implements, all painted white. The guests, of course, all came in white. Towards the end of the evening, there was a fight and one of the guests drove off with Elizabeth Pelly. The car crashed, and although she was unhurt, he was killed. At the inquest, it came out that the party was one long drunken brawl. Where parental and public disapproval had only encouraged their outlandish behaviour, this accident did much to sober the Bright Young People up.

The 'ancestors' of the Bright Young People were individualists, which made them, in a sense, Bohemians. Their successors courted publicity, although as their behaviour was 'newsworthy', they could hardly have avoided such attention from the Press. With such interest in them and their antics, it was the Press who eventually made the Bright Young People into a 'movement'; it made them significant, even important. What had started as a bright impulse, a lark ('We were all so over-excited', Loelia Ponsonby admitted), became a self-conscious crusade.

Part of the glamour of Bohemia is in its mystery. Advertised, it defeats its own object; organised, it becomes a contradiction in terms. English Society has always been conventional. For Society to come to terms with the defiant Bright Young People, with their pseudo-Bohemian manners and morals, was unthinkable. In just a few years, the younger generation's spontaneity and zest for life were replaced by their demand for total moral freedom and the right to shock. Their responsibility to their class, that is, good manners and other marks of birth, education and property, became a bore. The only virtue that they could claim was that at least they were not hypocrites.

Epilogue

*A*ND SO THAT LOST GENERATION came to the end of their Primrose Path. They had lived at a rate that was difficult to sustain, and so either burned themselves out or quietened down – as Sonia complained to Alastair in Waugh's *Black Mischief*: 'D'you know, deep down in my heart I've got a tiny fear that Basil [Seal] is going to turn serious on us too.'(1) Although their reckless spirit had been lost, their love of that luxurious life, which had become so deeply ingrained in Society, remained.

Throughout the decade, they had all lived in the shadow cast by the horrors of the First World War, and their reaction against it was to lead a totally self-indulgent, hedonistic, life. They danced through the depressions; the General Strike was a 'lark', and most were unaffected by the chronic unemployment and hunger marches. The old order kept up appearances, oblivious of the change around them. There were, of course, notable exceptions – men such as the young MP for Stockton, Captain Harold Macmillan, who cared deeply about the plight of their constituents. Society survived the Wall Street Crash in New York in 1929. Some even survived its 'knock-on' effect in London and the collapse of the financier, Clarence Hawtry, which precipitated the Stock Exchange slump. But the desperate state of the country was finally driven home when Britain was forced off the Gold Standard in the summer of 1931 and the value of the pound plummeted – 'the explosion in the dining-room when my father heard the news was just as violent as anything we had heard in the war!'(2) At that moment, the twenties were effectively ended, and the thirties had begun.

Source Notes

Introduction

1. Lord Byron, *The Age of Bronze*, 1823
2. G. Mingay, *English Landed Society in the 18th Century*, 1963, p. 86
3. Leonore Davidoff, *The Best Circles*, 1973, p. 20
4. Henry Francis Lyte, *Abide with me*, 1.7
5. Kenneth Rose *King George V*, 1983, p. 225
6. John Collier and Iain Lang, *Just the Other Day*, 1932, p. 36
7. Patrick Balfour, *Society Racket*, 1933, p. 51
8. Jessica Mitford, *Hons and Rebels*, 1961, p. 43
9. *Hansard*, House of Lords, Debate of 17 July 1922
10. Noreen Branson, *Britain in the 1920s*, 1975, p. 92

Chapter 1

1. Evelyn Waugh, *Brideshead Revisited*, 1951, p. 25
2. Ian Anstruther to the author
3. Waugh, p. 36
4. Lesley Lewis, *The Private Life of a Country House*, 1980, p. 45
5. Mrs John Dower in Merlin Waterstone (ed.), *The Country House Remembered*, 1985, p. 222
6. Loelia, Duchess of Westminster, *Grace and Favour*, 1961, p. 79
7. personal comment to the author
8. *ibid*
9. Mitford, pp. 8 and 9
10. *ibid*, p. 3
11. Patricia, Viscountess Hambledon in Waterstone, p. 225
12. personal comment to the author
13. Violet Powell, *Five out of Six*, 1960, p. 144
14. personal comment to the author
15. letter to the author
16. Mitford, (*Hons and Rebels*), p. 32
17. personal comment to the author
18. *ibid*
19. Ian Anstruther to the author
20. Diana Mosley, *A Life of Contrasts*, 1977, p. 28
21. letter to the author

22. The Hon. Mrs Ashley-Cooper in letter to the author
23. Mrs Richard Cavendish in Waterstone, p. 208
24. Lord Egremont, *Wyndham and Children First*, 1961, p. 60

Chapter 2

1. letter to the author
2. Mrs Elaine Goldwater in *The Sunday Times*, 30 September, 1984
3. Evelyn Waugh, *Decline and Fall*, 1928, p. 16
4. letter to the author
5. Richard Ollard, *An English Education*, 1982, p. 11
6. *ibid*, p. 11
7. *ibid*, p. 12
8. Waugh, (*Brideshead*), p. 33
9. John Masters, *Pilgrim Son*, 1971, p. 281
10. letter to the author
11. Lord Home, *The Way the Wind Blows*, 1976, pp. 26 and 27
12. Henry Green, *Pack My Bag*, 1940, pp. 108 and 109
13. personal comment to the author
14. Cyril Connolly, *Enemies of Promise*, 1938, p. 280
15. Michael Astor, *Tribal Feeling*, 1963, p. 98
16. Ollard, p. 163
17. *ibid*, p. 147
18. Connolly, p. 302
19. William Douglas Home, *Half-Term Report*, 1954, p. 35
20. Christopher Hollis, *Along the Road to Frome*, 1958, p. 44
21. Astor, p. 98
22. Home, p. 31
23. Ollard, p. 141
24. Home, p. 35

Chapter 3

1. Balfour, p. 61
2. Green, p. 204
3. Waugh, (*Brideshead*), p. 23
4. Hollis, p. 65
5. Evelyn Waugh, *A Little Learning*, 1964, p. 173

6. Waugh, (*Learning*), p. 172
7. The Marquess of Bath to the author
8. personal comment to the author
9. *ibid*
10. Green, p. 201
11. *ibid*, p. 201
12. *ibid*, p. 208
13. Waugh, (*Learning*), p. 179
14. Christopher Sykes, *Evelyn Waugh*, 1975, p. 48
15. Balfour, p. 62
16. Harold Acton, *Diary of an Aesthete*, 1948, p. 122
17. Waugh, (*Learning*), p. 179
18. Ed. Marie-Jacqueline Lancaster, *Brian Howard, Portrait of a Failure*, 1968, p. 177
19. John Fothergill, *An Innkeeper's Diary*, 1931, pp. 21 and 22
20. Acton, p. 124
21. Lancaster, p. 215
22. *ibid*, p. 215
23. Mitford, p. 23
24. Waugh, (*Decline*), 1928, p. 10
25. Lancaster, p. 186
26. *Oxford Chronicle*, 19 February 1927
27. Lancaster, p. 144
28. *Oxford Chronicle*, 19 February 1927
29. Lancaster, p. 176
30. Fothergill, p. 61
31. Daphne Fielding, *Mercury Presides*, 1954, p. 107
32. Beverley Nichols, *The Sweet and Twenties*, 1958, p. 121
33. *ibid*, p. 122

Chapter 4

1. Walter Bagehot, *The English Constitution*, 1929, p. 46
2. Henry Channon, diary entry 14 May 1924
3. *ibid*
4. personal comment to the author
5. HRH The Duke of Windsor, *The King's Story*, 1951, p. 234
6. personal comment to the author
7. Windsor, p. 163
8. Beverley Nichols, *The Unforgiving Minute*, 1978, pp. 115 and 116
9. Henry Channon, diary entry 4 June 1923
10. personal comment to the author
11. Lady Troubridge, *The Book of Etiquette*, 1926, p. 154
12. Jennifer Ellis (ed.), *Thatched with Gold, the Memoirs of Mabell, Countess of Airlie*, 1962, p. 143

13. Viscount Sandhurst, *From Day to Day*, II, 1929, p. 343
14. John Montgomery, *The Twenties*, 1957, p. 165
15. Lewis, p. 112
16. personal comment to the author
17. *ibid*
18. Violet Powell, *Five out of Six*, 1960, p. 74
19. *ibid*, p. 53
20. Fielding, p. 84
21. Sykes, p. 251
22. personal comment to the author
23. letter to the author
24. Westminster, (*Grace and Favour*), p. 87
25. Lady Mary Clive, *Brought up and Brought out*, 1938, p. 198
26. Fielding, p. 87
27. Clive, p. 188
28. Westminster, p. 85
29. Clive, p. 192
30. Westminster, p. 87
31. personal comment to the author
32. Alison Adburgham, *A Punch History of Manners and Modes*, 1961, p. 306
33. *ibid*, p. 306
34. Balfour, p. 130
35. *ibid*, p. 133
36. *ibid*, p. 133

Chapter 5

1. personal comment to the author
2. Clive, p. 186
3. letter to the author
4. *The Times*, 29 November 1918
5. Airlie, p. 159
6. Dorothy Laird, *Royal Ascot*, 1976, pp. 188 and 189
7. *ibid*, p. 189
8. *ibid*, p. 189
9. *The Times*, 21 June 1924
10. *The Times*, 19 June 1925
11. Lt.-Col. A. A. Duff, *The Graphic*, 15 May 1920
12. *Country Life*, 12 June 1920
13. Colonel Richard Hanmer to author
14. *Country Life*, 12 June 1920
15. Balfour, p. 59
16. F. S. Ashley-Cooper, *Country Life*, 15 July 1922
17. Home, p. 33
18. Hans Duffy, *In England Now*, 1932, p. 229
19. H. W. Austin, *Lawn Tennis Bits and Pieces*, 1930, p. 64
20. Suzanne Lenglen, *Lawn Tennis for Girls*, 1922, p. 38

21. R. D. Burnell, *Henley Regatta*, 1957, p. 41
22. F. Hecksall-Smith, *Sacred Cowes*, 1939, p. 81
23. *ibid*, p. 82
24. Noël Coward, *Private Lives*, 1930

Chapter 6

1. Balfour, p. 256
2. Report of the Departmental Committee on Tenant Farmers and Sales of Estates, *Parliamentary Papers* XLVII
3. *The Times*, 21 April 1922
4. Central Landowner's Association, *Quarterly Circular*, February 1922, pp. 5 and 6
5. Balfour, p. 258
6. *The Times*, 19 May 1920
7. C. F. G. Masterman, *England after the War*, 1922, p. 31
8. Nancy Mitford, *The Blessing*, 1951, p. 194
9. Evelyn Waugh, *A Handful of Dust*, 1934, p. 18
10. Mitford, *(The Blessing)*, p. 194
11. Bedford, p. 17
12. personal comment to the author
13. Graves and Hodge, p. 186
14. Nancy Mitford, *Love in a Cold Climate*, 1949, p. 45
15. letter to the author
16. Duffy, p. 1
17. Wyndham, p. 61
18. Hambledon, p. 63
19. *ibid*, p. 63
20. Fielding, *(Mercury Presides)*, p. 99
21. personal comment to the author
22. *ibid*
23. Wyndham, p. 61
24. Philip Ziegler, *Diana Cooper*, 1981, p. 155
25. Fielding, p. 111
26. personal comment to the author
27. Hambledon, p. 63
28. Mitford, *(The Blessing)*, p. 151
29. Robert Graves and Alan Hodge, *The Long Weekend*, 1940, p. 131
30. *Punch*, 14 December 1923
31. Nichols, *(Sweet and Twenties)*, p. 134
32. Anne, Countess of Rosse in Waterstone, p. 69
33. Mowat, p. 202
34. Beaton, p. 154
35. personal comment to the author
36. *ibid*

Chapter 7

1. Simon Blow, *Fields Elysian*, 1983, p. 53
2. Waugh, *(Brideshead)*, p. 157
3. Miss Monica Sheriffe to the author
4. Sykes, p. 116
5. personal comment to the author
6. Nicholas Courtney, *Sporting Royals*, 1983, pp. 21 and 22
7. letter to the author
8. Miss Monica Sherriffe to the author
9. personal comment to the author
10. Blow, p. 112
11. Miss Monica Sheriffe to the author
12. Egremont, p. 63
13. The Hon. Douglas Cairns, *Letters of Young Sportsmen, The Country Life*, 1920, p. 287
14. personal comment to the author
15. Major the Hon. John Ashley-Cooper to the author
16. *ibid*
17. Beckwith, p. 29
18. personal comment to the author
19. The Duke of Richmond and Gordon to the author
20. Evelyn Waugh, *Vile Bodies*, 1930, p. 158
21. The Duke of Richmond and Gordon to the author
22. Courtney, p. 183
23. Balfour, p. 106
24. *Morning Post*, 23 June 1927

Chapter 8

1. Balfour, p. 124
2. *ibid*, pp. 125 and 126
3. Brian Masters, *Great Hostesses*, 1982, p. 50
4. *ibid*, p. 1
5. W. C. Sellar and R. J. Yeatman, *1066 And All That*, 1930, p. 62
6. Nichols, *(Sweet and Twenties)*, p. 80
7. Masters, p. 88
8. Osbert Sitwell, *Left Hand, Right Hand*, 1944, p. 109
9. Masters, p. 87
10. *ibid*, p. 111
11. Balfour, p. 135
12. Masters, p. 109
13. Channon, p. 106
14. Fielding, p. 136
15. Masters, p. 109
16. Kenneth Clarke in Masters, p. 134
17. *ibid*, p. 134
18. *ibid*, p. 139
19. Nichols, *(Sweet and Twenties)*, p. 157

20. Daphne Fielding, *Emerald and Nancy*, 1965, p. 101
21. Kenneth Clark in Masters, p. 153
22. *ibid*, p. 158
23. *ibid*, p. 163
24. Nichols, (*Sweet and Twenties*), 159
25. *ibid*, p. 158
26. Masters, p. 154
27. *ibid*, p. 154
28. Fielding, p. 102
29. *ibid*, p. 207
30. *ibid*, pp. 100 and 101
31. *ibid*, p. 101
32. *ibid*, p. 206
33. *ibid*, p. 100
34. Masters, p. 199

Chapter 9

1. Balfour, p. 176
2. Waugh, (*Brideshead*), p. 118
3. Balfour, p. 160
4. *ibid*, p. 161
5. *Daily Sketch*, 17 April 1927
6. personal comment to the author
7. Graves and Hodge, p. 43
8. Waugh, (*Vile Bodies*), p. 80
9. Nerina Shute, *We Mixed our Drinks*, 1945, p. 11
10. Nichols, (*Sweet and Twenties*), p. 109
11. *ibid*, p. 109
12. Collier and Lang, p. 201
13. *ibid*, p. 209
14. personal comment to the author
15. Graves and Hodge, p. 101
16. Waugh, (*Vile Bodies*), p. 130
17. Collier and Lang, p. 156
18. Adburgham, p. 283
19. Nichols, (*Sweet and Twenties*), p. 129
20. Balfour, p. 140
21. Adburgham, p. 283
22. Nichols, (*Sweet and Twenties*), pp. 132 and 133
23. *ibid*, p. 126
24. Arlem, p. 111
25. Graves and Hodge, p. 179
26. Collier and Lang, p. 155
27. Balfour, p. 142
28. *Punch*, 1926
29. Westminster, p. 81
30. *ibid*, p. 81
31. Arlen, p. 42
32. Nichols, (*Sweet and Twenties*), p. 135
33. Fielding, p. 99
34. *The Weekly Dispatch*, 18 January 1925
35. *Punch*, February 1929
36. Collier and Lang, p. 149
37. *ibid*, p. 150
38. Graves and Hodge, p. 49

Chapter 10

1. Richard Aldington, *Death of a Hero*, 1929, p. 63
2. *Daily Mail*, 23 February 1919
3. Graves and Hodge, p. 38
4. Balfour, p. 108
5. C. E. M. Joad, *Under the Fifth Rib*, 1946, p. 21
6. *Punch*, April 1923
7. Arlen, p. 42
8. Fielding, p. 106
9. Leslie Bailey, *Scrapbook of the Twenties*, 1959, p. 63
10. Waugh, (*Brideshead*), pp. 110 and 111
11. Jack Glicco, *Madness after Midnight*, 1960, p. 132
12. Graves and Hodge, p. 121
13. Kate Meyrick, *Secrets of the 43 Club*, 1933, p. 192
14. Adburgham, p. 289
15. Fielding, p. 121
16. Hugo Vickers, *Cocktails and Laughter*, 1983, p. 12
17. Arlen, p. 111
18. Catalogue of W. A. Gilby's Centenary Exhibition, 1952

Chapter 11

1. personal comment to the author
2. Ralph Nevill, *The World of Fashion*, 1927, p. 74
3. Duke of Richmond and Gordon to the author
4. Clive, pp. 200 and 201
5. personal comment to the author
6. Balfour, p. 122
7. Waugh, (*Brideshead*), p. 194
8. Airlie, pp. 177 and 178
9. Nichols, (*Sweet and Twenties*), pp. 176 and 177
10. *Illustrated London News*, 15 May 1926
11. The Marquess of Bath to the author
12. *Illustrated London News*, 15 May 1926
13. H. W. Austin, *Lawn Tennis Bits and Pieces*, 1930, p. 94
14. Collier and Lang, *Just the Other Day*, 1932, p. 188
15. *Illustrated London News*, 15 May 1926
16. Grantley, p. 137
17. *ibid*, p. 137
18. Waugh, (*Brideshead*, p. 198
19. Airlie, p. 177
20. *Daily Mail*, 8 May 1926
21. Christopher Isherwood, *Lions and Shadows*, 1933, p. 121

Chapter 12

1. James Laver (ed.), *Between the Wars*, 1961, pp. 118 and 119 (Jacques Reval, *The Woman of 1926*)
2. Westminster, p. 122
3. *ibid*, p. 119
4. Lord Birkenhead, *Lady Eleanor Smith*, 1953, p. 61
5. *ibid*, p. 61
6. *ibid*, p. 62
7. Balfour, p. 167
8. *Sunday Dispatch*, 22 July 1929
9. Mosley, p. 86
10. Balfour, p. 168
11. *ibid*, p. 168
12. *The Dragoman's* (Tom Driberg) column, *Daily Express*, 23 July 1929
13. Mosley, p. 86
14. *The Dragoman, Daily Express*, 23 July 1929
15. Mosley, p. 87
16. Birkenhead, p. 59
17. Westminster, pp. 120 and 121
18. Ziegler, p. 167
19. Westminster, p. 121
20. *Daily Mail*, 26 July 1924
21. The Marquess of Bath to the author
22. Fielding, p. 72
23. Westminster, p. 122
24. Birkenhead, p. 59
25. Waugh, (*Vile Bodies*), p. 123
26. Lancaster, p. 269
27. *ibid*, pp. 267 and 268
28. Mary Craig, *Longford*, 1978, p. 37
29. Lancaster, p. 269
30. *Daily Express*, 21 July 1928
31. Corisande, *Evening Standard*, 3 March 1929
32. *ibid*
33. Westminster, p. 110
34. Tom Driberg quoted in Lancaster, pp. 229 and 230
35. Lancaster, p. 230
36. *ibid*, pp. 264 and 265
37. *Daily Express*, 14 July 1928
38. Lancaster, p. 266
39. *Sunday Chronicle*, 15 July 1928
40. *ibid*
41. Cecil Beaton, *The Glass of Fashion*, 1954, p. 59
42. Westminster, p. 122
43. Balfour, p. 170
44. *Daily News*, 1928
45. *Daily Express*, 1929
46. F. R. Holmes, repeated in Laver, pp. 118 and 119
47. Lancaster, p. 266

Epilogue

1. Evelyn Waugh, *Black Mischief*, 1932, pp. 296 and 297
2. personal comment to the author

INDEX